XML
WEB SERVICES
IN THE
ORGANIZATION

Chris Boar

PUBLISHED BY
Microsoft Press
A Division of Microsoft Corporation
One Microsoft Way
Redmond, Washington 98052-6399

Library of Congress Cataloging-in-Publication Data
Boar, Chris, 1968-
    XML Web services in the organization / Chris Boar.
        p. cm.
    ISBN 0-7356-1882-8
    1. XML (Document markup language)   2. Internet programming.   I. Title.

    QA76.76.H94B63   2003
    005.2'76--dc21   2003046487

Printed and bound in the United States of America.

1 2 3 4 5 6 7 8 9   QWE   8 7 6 5 4 3

Distributed in Canada by H.B. Fenn and Company Ltd.

A CIP catalogue record for this book is available from the British Library.

Microsoft Press books are available through booksellers and distributors worldwide. For further information about international editions, contact your local Microsoft Corporation office or contact Microsoft Press International directly at fax (425) 936-7329. Visit our Web site at www.microsoft.com/mspress. Send comments to *mspinput@microsoft.com*.

Acquisitions Editor: Anne Hamilton
Project Editor: Barbara Moreland
Technical Editor: Julie Xiao

Body Part No. X09-39006

Table of Contents

Acknowledgements

To my wife, Lynda, who encouraged, supported, and put up with me over the past year—thank you.

To my daughter Jessica; Daddy has finally finished his book. (A year is a long time when you're only 4.)

To my daughter Ashley, who joined us during the writing of this book. The timing was not ideal, but you slept really well. Thanks for that!

To the people at Microsoft Press, especially Barbara and Julie. I really appreciate all your hard work. Thanks.

Introduction

If you were asked for a list of important events in the history of information technology, you might include things such as the introduction of the personal computer, the graphical user interface, the mouse, and the Internet. I believe that XML-based Web services will, in time, be acknowledged as an equally important change in how we use, develop, and share applications and information.

When you have worked in the IT industry for some time, like I have, you get used to the innovation that constantly feeds its development. Occasionally, something really excites you, and for me Web services definitely falls into this rare category.

The interoperation problems that Web services solve are not only broad in technical terms but also broad in that almost all IT departments face these problems. I can think of countless applications I've worked on where various systems needed to be closely coupled, yet were based on different platforms. I can remember, too clearly, the pain I went through getting information back and forth between these systems; the tools available included flat files, e-mail attachments, binary formats, and data packets sent over TCP/IP. The final insult came five years ago when I had to implement electronic data interchange (EDI) between a number of trading partners and the large manufacturing company I worked for. So, when I originally read that Web services could help me avoid such painful experiences, I was very interested.

My interest in Web services was driven by two more facts. First, there was nothing particularly complicated about Web services. At the end of the day, Web services are XML data in the format of SOAP messages transported over some ubiquitous method (more often than not HTTP). I like simplicity because it means the technology is more likely to work, and simplicity can increase the speed of adoption. Second, Web services are well supported by the Microsoft Windows .NET Framework. Of course, there are numerous other development platforms for Web services on both Microsoft and non-Microsoft platforms, but it was the .NET Framework with which I originally explored Web services. What complexity there is, in terms of supporting the SOAP messages, is contained within the .NET Framework. You'll see in Chapter 6 that it's still possible to get into the messages when you need to, but most of the time, you can use and create Web services without having to get too deeply involved with the mechanics. What the .NET Framework does leave to you is the design of the Web service and how it fits into your applications.

About This Book

The purpose of this book is to identify situations in which organizations can use Web services to develop efficient, productive, and easily managed solutions to their business challenges and to demonstrate through example how these solutions can be implemented. Because almost any application made up of distributed functionality can benefit from Web services, the book focuses broadly on companies who use information technology to produce their product or services rather than those whose primary product is IT services.

The primary audiences for this book are system architects and software developers in the IT departments of the target organizations. The book assumes that you have a basic understanding of Microsoft .NET technologies. You need only a passing knowledge of XML-based Web services because the book introduces you gently to the details of Web services before moving into the sample problems and solutions.

The book's sample code is written in Microsoft Visual C# .NET. Some of the applications use Microsoft ADO.NET, Microsoft's latest incarnation of ActiveX Data Objects (ADO). The book is not a technical resource on ADO, and explanations of the features in ADO.NET used in the sample applications will be discussed as they arise. You'll find that the close integration of ADO.NET with XML is extremely useful in XML-based Web service applications. (Microsoft Press offers several books that cover ADO.NET extensively.)

Organization of This Book

Chapter 1 introduces XML-based Web services as developed within Microsoft Visual Studio .NET. In this chapter, you'll learn how to create, consume, and locate simple Web services.

Chapters 2 and 3 demonstrate how XML-based Web services can be used to solve two specific, potential internal trouble spots. Chapter 2 discusses the problems of supporting staff that work outside the corporate intranet. Having independent, mobile staff and having people work from a customer location are now common business situations. Ensuring that these workers are integrated into the corporate systems can be a challenge that Web services can help address.

Chapter 3 looks at how XML-based Web services can help with problems of bridging internal applications often caused by acquisitions and mergers. It's common for organizations to have a heterogeneous environment, but making systems work together within this environment is not always easy. Web services can be the answer.

Chapters 4 and 5 address communication with external partners. Chapter 4 covers business-to-business communication, sometimes referred to as EDI. Chapter 5 discusses two different approaches to customers. The first part of the chapter shows how to use a Web service to link your data indirectly to your customers through other companies. The second part of the chapter looks at using Web services to provide functionality to customers directly by using a smart device application developed using the Microsoft .NET Compact Framework.

Chapter 6 addresses security. It shows you how to secure your Web services using the cryptographic functions supplied within the .NET Framework: encryption, signing, authentication, and authorization.

Chapter 7 discusses monitoring and scaling. Designing and implementing a Web service isn't enough; you must also ensure that the Web service can be monitored and scaled as necessary. Finally, the chapter discusses the Global XML Web Services Architecture (GXA).

Web services is a young technology, and significant development work is taking place to make it easier to use and better able to address particular needs. Chapter 7 concludes with a look at what lies ahead for XML-based Web services.

Installing and Using the Sample Files

You can download the sample files from the book's Companion Content page on the Web by connecting to *http://www.microsoft.com/mspress/books/6534.asp*. You need approximately 15 MB of free disk space to install this book's sample files. To access the sample files, click Companion Content in the More Information menu box on the right side of the page. The Companion Content Web page will load, which includes a link for downloading the sample files and connecting to Microsoft Press Support. The download link opens an executable file containing a license agreement. To copy the sample files to your hard disk, click the link to run the executable and then accept the license agreement that's presented. Once the sample files are decompressed, the setup program runs a short configuration routine. The routine configures the necessary applications and virtual directories in Internet Information Services (IIS). The sample files can be found under C:\Microsoft Press\XMLWSOrg.

The companion content for this book also includes the installation routine for Microsoft Office XP Web Services Toolkit 2. After you have installed the companion content, you can find the installation routine at C:\Microsoft Press\XMLWSOrg\Microsoft Office XP Web Services Toolkit 2.

The solutions that are based on Microsoft Office XP applications use this toolkit to consume the necessary XML-based Web services. These tools offer great support for Web services. You can use them to build powerful Web service applications without having to develop a lot of complicated software, which allows you to concentrate on the higher-level aspects of the solution and to be more productive.

System Requirements

The Web services in this book are built using Microsoft .NET. Clients for the Web services are either .NET-based clients or Office XP clients. The minimum hardware requirements for this book are similar to those for Visual Studio .NET 2003.

Processor	450 megahertz (MHz) Pentium II-class processor,
	600 MHz Pentium III-class processor recommended
Operating system	Microsoft Windows Server 2003
	Windows XP Professional
	Windows 2000 Professional (Service Pack 3 or later required for installation)
	Windows 2000 Server (Service Pack 3 or later required for installation)
Memory	Windows Server 2003: 160 megabytes (MB) of RAM
	Windows XP Professional: 160 MB of RAM
	Windows 2000 Professional: 96 MB of RAM
	Windows 2000 Server: 192 MB of RAM
Hard disk	1 gigabyte (GB) of available space required on system drive; 3.3 GB of available space required on installation drive; additional 1.9 GB of available space required for optional MSDN documentation

The following software is required to run the applications included in the companion content.

Visual Studio .NET 2003 (includes the Microsoft .NET Framework version 1.1)	Professional, Enterprise Developer, or Enterprise Architect editions
Office XP	Specifically, Microsoft Word 2002

Corrections, Comments, and Help

Every effort has been made to ensure the accuracy of this book and the contents of the sample files. Microsoft Press provides corrections and additional content for its books through the World Wide Web at the following Web site:

http://microsoft.com/mspress/support

If you have problems, comments, or ideas regarding this book or the sample files, please send them to Microsoft Press.

Send e-mail messages to

mspinput@microsoft.com

Or send postal mail to

Microsoft Press
Attn: *XML Web Services in the Organization* Editor
One Microsoft Way
Redmond, WA 98052-6399

Please note that Microsoft Press does not offer product support for Visual Studio .NET.

Visit the Microsoft Press Web Site

You're also invited to visit the Microsoft Press Web site at the following location:

http://www.microsoft.com/mspress

You'll find descriptions for the complete line of Microsoft Press books, information about ordering titles, notices of special features and events, additional content for Microsoft Press books, and much more.

1

Understanding the Basics of XML-Based Web Services

Before you can look at any solutions that use XML-based Web services, you should determine whether they meet your organization's needs and have a basic understanding of how they work. When you move through the chapters that follow and examine each sample application, you'll find that many of the lower-level details of Web services are hidden from you by the tools that we'll use. Having these low-level details taken care of for you allows you to develop efficient applications much quicker. However, you still need to understand what's happening "under the hood." What you don't know can hurt you when something goes wrong.

Behind Web services lie a number of recognized standards such as SOAP, Web Services Description Language (WSDL), and, of course, XML. In this chapter, you'll be introduced to each standard as you work through some actual code from both the client side and the server side.

The examples in this chapter aren't exactly real-world; they're contrived to help you learn the details of how Web services work. More complex examples will be discussed in the chapters to follow when we start to look at business problems and the applications to solve them.

Deciding to Use Web Services

Solving any business problem begins with a clear understanding of the organization's needs as well as the tools available for addressing those needs. Web services can provide powerful and versatile solutions, but they aren't the best answer to every business problem. For instance, a processing overhead is incurred to support the serialization to and from the SOAP messages. In situations in which servers and clients share a common platform, for example, in Microsoft Windows, you might be able to provide a better solution with a protocol optimized for that platform. Deciding whether to implement a Web service does take an element of crystal ball gazing. You need to weigh the existing infrastructure and services and then consider any changes that might occur over the lifetime of the solution being proposed.

Designing any system involves the balancing of conflicting needs, performance against stability, and extensibility against manageability. Web services are commonly thought of as an Internet technology. Because of the nature of the Internet, you can't make assumptions about the clients or servers connecting to a service you develop. Therefore, it's clear that Web services could form part of an Internet solution. For an intranet solution, the need to use Web services is less clear. You should also consider whether a Web service can handle the bandwidth necessary for your application. Large quantities of data that need to be passed between machines very quickly might not be best suited to being sent through a Web service.

For example, suppose your company has asked you to design a time and attendance system. Your proposal will be compared to a number of "off-the-shelf" packages to see which best meets the company's needs. The system requirements include

- Personal identity cards that all employees will carry.

- Identity card readers, positioned at the major entrances and exits of the building.

- A central server to poll and store the data from the readers.

- Client software that allows reports to be run off the data stored in the central server.

- Clients and a server located on the corporate intranet.

In this situation, linking the clients to the server using Web services would be unnecessary. Because both the clients and the server are located within the corporate intranet, it's possible to use a protocol between these machines that's optimized for the client and server software being used. Also, the amount of data being transferred to satisfy a query could be large, and a protocol that can handle such loads more efficiently would be in order.

Now suppose an additional requirement is added to the specification of your time and attendance system: the data needs to be made available to an outsourced payroll company. Making information available to an external company is an ideal opportunity for a Web service. Using a Web service provides the following benefits:

- You are making functionality available, not just data, which allows you to add necessary logic on top of the data. For example, your code can query a vacation database and then provide the necessary data to the external company. You could provide an interface that allows the remote company to query for changes in the staff database.

- Your solution is not tied to any particular operating system or hardware. If you need to change to another company, you simply point them to your Discovery of Web services (DISCO) or WSDL documents and let them implement the consumption of the Web service on whatever platform they have.

Understanding the advantages of Web services allows you to determine when they are the appropriate answer to your communication needs. Two common problems for which Web services offer superior solutions are supporting remote or traveling staff and coordinating internal application operation. Chapter 2 addresses remote staff, and Chapter 3 covers application interoperation.

Getting Set Up

To understand the code and the concepts in this chapter, you'll need Microsoft Visual Studio .NET 2003 installed. If you've already downloaded and installed this book's sample files, the Web service that you'll access first is already installed. Now you're ready to write the code to consume this Web service.

Accessing a Web Service

To consume the Web service, you must first build an application from which you can access your Web service.

> **Note**   Instead of writing this application, you can open the solution located at Microsoft Press\XMLWSOrg\Chapter1\AccessXMLWeb-Service\ AccessXMLWebService.sln in Visual Studio .NET 2003.

Creating the Application

The following instructions take you step by step through using Visual Studio .NET 2003 to create a simple Microsoft Windows application that will use the Web service you just installed.

1. Start Visual Studio .NET 2003.

2. On the Start Page, click the Projects tab and then click New Project.

3. In the New Project window, under Project Types, click Visual C# Projects. (You could also choose Visual Basic Projects.)

4. Under Templates, click Windows Application.

5. In the Name box, type **AccessXMLWebService** and then click OK.

6. From the Toolbox, drag a button to Form1.cs.

7. In the Properties window, change the *Text* property of *button1* to **Consume XML Web Service**.

8. Expand the *Size* property of *button1*, and then change the *Width* property to **160**.

9. Double-click *button1* to switch to the code view.

Adding a Web Reference

To use the functionality contained by a remote Web service, you need to add a reference to it in your project. You'll do that first, and then I'll discuss what it achieves.

1. In the Solution Explorer window, right-click References and then click Add Web Reference.

2. In the Add Web Reference dialog box, in the URL box, type the URL **http://localhost/XMLWSOrg/Chapter1/UTCService/Time.asmx** and then press Enter.

> **Note** If you changed the installation defaults for the Web service during setup, you'll need to enter a different URL.

The left panel of the window should show the operations supported by the Time Web service. The right panel allows you to view some of the details of the Web service. For now, simply click Add Reference.

Although little has changed visually in the integrated development environment (IDE), a lot has happened in the background. The details of adding a Web reference will be examined later in this chapter; for now, you'll move on and write the code to use the Web service.

Looking on the Surface

If you display the Class View window in Visual Studio (on the View menu, click Class View), under the *AccessXMLWebService* namespace, you'll see the *Form1* class and the *localhost* namespace. Expand the *localhost* namespace, and then expand the *Time* class. *Time* supports a number of methods, one of which is *UTCTime*.

The code to call the *UTCTime* method in the *button1_Click* procedure is straightforward; simply add the following:

```
localhost.Time timeWebService = new localhost.Time();
MessageBox.Show(timeWebService.UTCTime());
```

Now you can test this incredibly simple application. Press F5 to start. In the Form1 window, click Consume XML Web Service. Wait a second or two, and a message box will appear with the local time of the server that holds the Web service in Universal Coordinated Time (UTC).

Implementing the Web service in this test application is about as easy as it gets. The method you called took no parameters, and the data returned was a simple string. In later chapters, the Web services you develop to solve business problems will involve more complex operations.

Looking Under the Hood

Now we can rewind to the beginning and examine just what happened to make this simple application and its interaction with the Web service work. First you added a Web reference to the project. You entered the URL to the Web service you wanted to use in the Add Web Reference dialog box in Visual Studio .NET 2003. For Visual Studio to make this Web service available for you to use, Visual Studio must obtain information about the capabilities of the Web service.

To get this information, Visual Studio .NET 2003 requests the discovery document from the Web service using the URL *http://localhost/XMLWSOrg/Chapter1/UTCService/Time.asmx?DISCO*. The following code shows the returned document:

```
<?xml version="1.0" encoding="utf-8" ?>
<discovery xmlns:xsd="http://www.w3.org/2001/XMLSchema"
  xmlns:xsi="http://www.w3.org/2001/XMLSchema-instance"
  xmlns="http://schemas.xmlsoap.org/disco/">
  <contractRef
    ref="http://localhost/XMLWSOrg/Chapter1/UTCService/Time.asmx?wsdl"
    docRef="http://localhost/XMLWSOrg/Chapter1/UTCService/Time.asmx"
    xmlns="http://schemas.xmlsoap.org/disco/scl/" />
  <soap address="http://localhost/XMLWSOrg/Chapter1/UTCService/Time.asmx"
    xmlns:q1="http://fabrikam.com/XMLWSOrg/" binding="q1:TimeSoap"
    xmlns="http://schemas.xmlsoap.org/disco/soap/" />
</discovery>
```

This discovery document provides information on the operations supported by the Web service. Notice the *ContractRef* element. This particular discovery document has only one *ContractRef* element, and it contains the URL of the WSDL description of the Web service: *http://localhost/XMLWSOrg/Chapter1/UTCService/Time.asmx?wsdl*.

Introducing WSDL

Visual Studio .NET 2003 uses the WSDL document to get the information it needs on how to interact with the operation of the Web service. The WSDL document is shown in the following code, which you can test yourself by launching a Web browser and typing in the URL **http://localhost/XMLWSOrg/Chapter1/UTC-Service/Time.asmx?wsdl**:

```
<?xml version="1.0" encoding="utf-8" ?>
<definitions xmlns:http="http://schemas.xmlsoap.org/wsdl/http/"
  xmlns:soap="http://schemas.xmlsoap.org/wsdl/soap/"
  xmlns:s="http://www.w3.org/2001/XMLSchema"
  xmlns:s0="http://fabrikam.com/XMLWSOrg/"
  xmlns:soapenc="http://schemas.xmlsoap.org/soap/encoding/"
  xmlns:tm="http://microsoft.com/wsdl/mime/textMatching/"
  xmlns:mime="http://schemas.xmlsoap.org/wsdl/mime/"
  targetNamespace="http://fabrikam.com/XMLWSOrg/"
  xmlns="http://schemas.xmlsoap.org/wsdl/">
  <types>
    <s:schema elementFormDefault="qualified"
```

```
        targetNamespace="http://fabrikam.com/XMLWSOrg/">
          <s:element name="UTCTime">
            <s:complexType />
          </s:element>
          <s:element name="UTCTimeResponse">
            <s:complexType>
              <s:sequence>
                <s:element minOccurs="0" maxOccurs="1"
                  name="UTCTimeResult" type="s:string" />
              </s:sequence>
            </s:complexType>
          </s:element>
      </s:schema>
    </types>
    <message name="UTCTimeSoapIn">
      <part name="parameters" element="s0:UTCTime" />
    </message>
    <message name="UTCTimeSoapOut">
      <part name="parameters" element="s0:UTCTimeResponse" />
    </message>
    <portType name="TimeSoap">
        <operation name="UTCTime">
          <input message="s0:UTCTimeSoapIn" />
          <output message="s0:UTCTimeSoapOut" />
        </operation>
    </portType>
    <binding name="TimeSoap" type="s0:TimeSoap">
      <soap:binding transport="http://schemas.xmlsoap.org/soap/http"
        style="document" />
      <operation name="UTCTime">
        <soap:operation soapAction="http://fabrikam.com/XMLWSOrg/UTCTime"
          style="document" />
        <input>
          <soap:body use="literal" />
        </input>
        <output>
          <soap:body use="literal" />
        </output>
      </operation>
    </binding>
    <service name="Time">
      <port name="TimeSoap" binding="s0:TimeSoap">
        <soap:address location=
          "http://localhost/XMLWSOrg/Chapter1/UTCService/Time.asmx" />
      </port>
    </service>
</definitions>
```

> **More Info**   For more information on WSDL, go to *http://www.w3.org /TR/wsdl*. For additional background information, read "Don Box on the Importance of Being WSDL" at *http://msdn.microsoft.com/library /default.asp?url=/library/en-us/dnwsdl/html/boxwsdl.asp*. The WSDL specification page can be found at *http://msdn.microsoft.com/library /default.asp?url=/library/en-us/dnwsdl/html/wsdlspecindex.asp*.

Finding the Proxy Code

Let's pause for a moment and consider how your code interacted with the Web service. In your code, you actually created an instance of a class and then called one of its methods. You wrote no code that sent or received messages over the network. In fact, you played no part in the formatting of data or actually sending it over the network, but in this case, you accessed a Web service that was local.

Figure 1-1 summarizes your knowledge of this system at the moment. You used some simple code in your form to get to the functionality of the Web service. The gap between the simple code and the Web service is closed by code that creates a local proxy class for the remote Web service generated by Visual Studio .NET using information contained in the downloaded WSDL document.

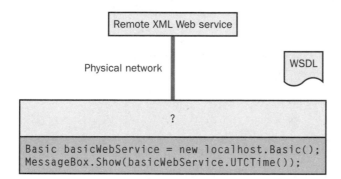

Figure 1-1   Current understanding of the system

If you have followed along in Visual Studio .NET 2003, make sure you can see the Solution Explorer window and then click Show All Files on the Project menu. Now the hidden files included in the solution are displayed in the Solution Explorer window. Expand the Web References node, then the localhost node, and then the Reference.map file. You'll see a file named Reference.cs (or Reference.vb if you're developing with Visual Basic .NET 2003). If you open this file, you'll see the proxy code that connects the two simple lines of code to the remote Web service.

Creating the Proxy Code

The proxy code doesn't do all the work. The Microsoft Windows .NET Framework provides most of the code needed to allow you to consume this remote Web service. The code in the Reference.cs file is the code that must be generated to support this particular Web service. This code is generated for you by a program named WSDL.exe, using the information contained in the WSDL file downloaded from the remote Web service. If you're writing your application using Notepad and the .NET Framework, you would need to run WSDL.exe manually. If you're using Visual Studio .NET 2003, this code is generated for you in the background. By the way, you normally don't need to change the code in the Reference.cs (or Reference.vb) file. If you do change it and you use the Update Web Reference command, the code will be regenerated.

The Complete Picture

Figure 1-2 fills in the missing pieces. Now it should be clearer how all this work happened with so little code.

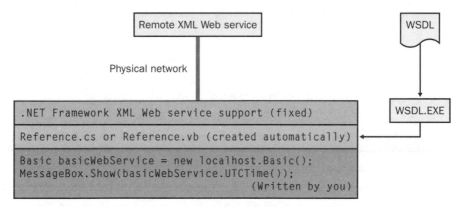

Figure 1-2   Completed understanding of the system

At this stage, you should have successfully accessed a Web service. You should understand how it's possible to do so with only a few lines of code. The .NET Framework allows you to consider a remote Web service as a local class. A considerable amount of processing is taking place behind the scenes. To be able to develop efficient Web services and fix problems when they don't work, you need to understand the "hidden" details.

Looking Behind the Scenes

The best way to understand the hidden details of your Web service is to look at the data itself using the SOAP Trace Utility that ships with the Soap Toolkit 3.0. After you install the Soap Toolkit 3.0, the tool appears under the Program group as Microsoft SOAP Toolkit Version 3 with a shortcut named Trace Utility. This utility allows you to peek into the requests and responses between your client and the Web service.

> **Note**   If you don't have the Soap Toolkit Version 3.0 installed on your machine, you can download it from the MSDN Library at *http://msdn.microsoft.com/library/default.asp?url=/downloads/list/websrv.asp*.

First you need to reconfigure your client to send its requests to a TCP/IP port that will be monitored by the Trace utility. Once this reconfiguration is complete, you can run the client application again and view the messages in the Trace utility. Follow these steps to complete the reconfiguration:

1. Open the AccessXMLWebService application you wrote earlier if it's not already open in Visual Studio .NET 2003.

2. On the Project menu, verify that Show All Files is selected.

3. In the Solution Explorer window, expand Web References, expand localhost, expand Reference.map, and then open the file Reference.cs (or Reference.vb).

4. Scroll through the file until you come to a line that contains *this.Url*. Change the host name from *localhost* to **localhost:8080**.

5. Now start the Trace utility, if you haven't already.

6. In the MSSoapT window, on the File menu, point to New and then click Formatted Trace.

7. In the Trace Setup window, make sure that Local Port is set to 8080 and Destination Port is set to 80.

8. Make sure that Destination Host is set to localhost. Click OK.

9. Now switch back to Visual Studio .NET 2003, and press F5 to start the application.

10. Click the Consume XML Web Service button. It might take a little longer to show up this time, but the time of the Web service server (in UTC) should be displayed in a message box.

11. Switch back to the Trace utility. In the left panel of the trace window there should be a single entry of 127.0.0.1 (localhost). Expand this entry. Click the entry Message #1 beneath this IP address.

Now you should be able to see two XML documents, one in the upper-right pane and another in the lower-right pane. The upper pane contains the request to the Web service for the result of the operation named *UTCTime*.

```xml
<?xml version="1.0" encoding="utf-8" ?>
  <soap:Envelope xmlns:soap="http://schemas.xmlsoap.org/soap/envelope/"
    xmlns:xsi="http://www.w3.org/2001/XMLSchema-instance"
    xmlns:xsd="http://www.w3.org/2001/XMLSchema">
    <soap:Body>
      <UTCTime xmlns="http://fabrikam.com/XMLWSOrg/" />
    </soap:Body>
  </soap:Envelope>
```

The lower pane contains the response from the Web service, in this case, the time on the server.

```xml
<?xml version="1.0" encoding="utf-8" ?>
  <soap:Envelope xmlns:soap="http://schemas.xmlsoap.org/soap/envelope/"
    xmlns:xsi="http://www.w3.org/2001/XMLSchema-instance"
    xmlns:xsd="http://www.w3.org/2001/XMLSchema">
    <soap:Body>
      <UTCTimeResponse xmlns="http://fabrikam.com/XMLWSOrg/">
        <UTCTimeResult>4/10/2003 3:29:37 AM</UTCTimeResult>
      </UTCTimeResponse>
    </soap:Body>
  </soap:Envelope>
```

Clearly, both of the documents are XML, but more important, both of these documents are SOAP messages.

Understanding SOAP

SOAP is a lightweight XML-based protocol for exchanging structured and typed information. SOAP is the ingredient that allows you to use functionality on remote machines without needing to know anything specific about those machines. In Web services, XML is used for representing the data. That data still needs to have a common schema, and that schema is defined by SOAP.

More Info   For more information on SOAP, go to *http://www.w3.org /TR/SOAP*. Developer resources for SOAP can be found at *http: //msdn.microsoft.com/library/default.asp?url=/nhp/Default.asp? contentid=28000523*. To see the SOAP specification page, go to *http://msdn.microsoft.com/library/default.asp?url=/library/en-us /dnsoapspec/html/soapspecindex.asp?frame=true*.

SOAP Messages

SOAP is actually very simple. The SOAP specification splits a SOAP message into four parts. Only one of these parts is mandatory—the SOAP envelope used for encapsulating the message. The other three parts of a SOAP message are optional. The second part describes application-defined data types. The third part describes a request/response message exchange pattern called remote procedure call (RPC). (Most of the examples in this book access functionality of remote objects in an RPC-style way; however, this style is not a requirement of SOAP.) It's possible for a SOAP message to proceed to a server and have data processed or added to it before moving on to other nodes in its path. The fourth part of a SOAP message, which is also optional, defines a binding between SOAP and HTTP. You'll learn more about transport protocols in the following sections.

In the SOAP response message, you can see that you still have the SOAP *Envelope* element and the SOAP *Body* element. The XML within the SOAP *Body* element describes the data as being the *UTCTime* result.

In the WSDL file for the basic Web service shown earlier in this chapter, you find an element named *Types*. Within *Types*, you can see that *UTCTime* contains no *complexTypes*, meaning that there are no parameters to this operation. Under *UTCTimeResponse*, you have a single *complexType* named *UTCTimeResult* that is of type *string*. Hopefully, the fact that the method takes no parameters and returns a single parameter makes some sense when you look at the SOAP request and response messages. Remember that Visual Studio .NET 2003 uses the WSDL document to make the methods supported by Web services available to your code.

The Role of HTTP

Your knowledge of the illustrated system so far should be that a WSDL document describes the Web service and that SOAP is the specification of the message in the requests and responses that are presented in XML. If the client and Web service server are on different machines, data is carried over the network using HTTP. Remember that the goal of a Web service is to make its functionality available to all clients. HTTP is an Internet standard that's not tied to any particular hardware or software platform, so it helps the Web service meet this goal. HTTP actually works well when using SOAP in an RPC request/response style because HTTP itself is a stateless request/response mechanism. However, SOAP doesn't specify which transport you should use to move the message from point A to point B, and in some cases, other transports might be preferable. However, the majority of all Web services currently implemented run over HTTP.

Choosing Alternative SOAP Transports

Choices for SOAP transports include HTTP, Simple Mail Transport Protocol (SMTP), File Transport Protocol (FTP), and even a floppy disk. For those of you who aren't familiar with these alternatives to HTTP, let's start with SMTP.

Simple Mail Transfer Protocol

SMTP is at the heart of Internet e-mail. HTTP was designed as a stateless protocol used by clients to request documents from Web servers, and SMTP is a host-to-host protocol for the forwarding of e-mail messages. It's possible to attach a SOAP message to an e-mail message and send it to one or more recipients using SMTP. This protocol might be useful for devices that don't have permanent access to the Internet. A message can be created and "sent" even though it sits in the outbox waiting for the network to become available some time later.

File Transfer Protocol

FTP is an early, but still commonly used, Internet protocol for copying files from one machine to another. The files copied could be SOAP-formatted messages. FTP might be an alternative if a server is unable to support HTTP.

Floppy Disk

A SOAP message also can be saved to a smart card, a CD-ROM, or even a floppy disk. The media could then be given to someone else who would be able to open and read the SOAP message. Extreme security is likely the primary (or only) reason to implement SOAP using such "physical" transport. For example, you might have a server that you simply do not want making any network connection to any other network. You might then batch up SOAP messages, drop them onto a disk, and walk to another server that takes the SOAP messages from the disk and sends them on to their destination.

Now you understand SOAP, WSDL, and various transports over which you can send your SOAP-formatted messages. What remains is how you locate the URL of a particular Web service you want to access.

Using Directories to Locate Web Services

Directories have been established to provide central locations that allow developers to publish the details of their Web services. One site I check frequently is *www.salcentral.com*. If you haven't browsed such a Web service directory, try it. You'll be amazed at both the number and variety of Web services that have been developed and are freely available. However, before you start committing your next project to using some of these, be careful to check the status of the Web service. You should make sure that the Web service is only a test service. You should also make sure that the company hosting the service intends to keep it running for the duration of your project. Finally, you should consider whether the service can scale to meet the requirements of your application. In some respects, paying for access to a Web service might actually be a better proposition than creating your own because you can expect to get a service agreement with it.

Universal Description, Discovery, and Integration

Universal Description, Discovery, and Integration (UDDI) is a directory implemented as a Web service to allow developers to locate Web services either via an interface or programmatically. Initially started by Ariba, Microsoft, and IBM, its use is now being led by a group of industry leaders.

Using UDDI at Run Time

One of the concepts behind UDDI is helping developers address the issue of reliability in applications consuming Web services. For example, you might develop an application that utilizes a Web service from another company. Everything is functioning correctly until the remote server fails. To correct the problem, the company moves the Web service to a different server. Sadly, your application is hard-coded against the URL for your Web service. Although it's possible with DNS to change the IP address associated with a particular server name, that might not always be an option. When your application makes a call to the remote Web service that fails, your application could query the UDDI registry to see whether the URL for the Web service has changed. If it has changed, the application could bind to the new location and update its records accordingly. Of course, if the URL has not been updated, you still have a problem.

> **More Info**   In November 2001, the UDDI project released UDDI version 2 beta. Hewlett-Packard, IBM, Microsoft, and SAP have released version 2 beta implementations of their UDDI sites. For more information on UDDI, visit *http://www.uddi.org*, *http://uddi.microsoft.com*, and *http://www.ibm.com/services/uddi*. For developer resources, go to *http://msdn.microsoft.com/uddi*.

Publishing Web Services

The decision to publish your Web services with a directory depends on your business. If your customers and suppliers are relatively few with relationships that are closely maintained and developed, publishing your Web services might not be necessary. Any Web services that you want to share with these partners can be done informally. If you have a large number of customers, especially if your customers tend to find you rather than you finding them, publishing your Web services will help your customers locate your product or services.

You've now accessed a Web service and taken a high-level view of each of the components that makes it possible. This first example Web service was about as simple as it can get. The Web services in later chapters will deal with more complex data needs. The next step is to progress to the server side and to create a Web service (again using Visual Studio .NET 2003).

Developing a Web Service

You will now develop a new Web service. You'll use an imaginary company, Fabrikam, Inc. Your customers have asked to be able to query your stock levels by part number. Therefore, this Web service needs to accept a part number and return a stock level for that part number. If the part number specified is unknown, it will return a 0 stock level. If this were a real Web service, you would query a database for the stock level or perhaps request this information from a business object. In the example Web service, the part numbers and stock levels are all hard-coded.

This Web service is provided in this book's sample files. You can open the solution in Visual Studio .NET from Microsoft Press\XMLWSOrg\Chapter1\Stock-WebService\StockWebService.sln.

Code Inside a Web Service

Open the inventory.asmx file to see the example Web service. (.asmx is the extension given to ASP.NET Web service files.) The code for this Web service, shown in the following code listing, is contained in a dependent, code-behind file named inventory.asmx.cs (or inventory.asmx.vb). When you develop in Visual Studio .NET 2003, you don't need to worry about these code-behind files because when you select Code View on the inventory.asmx file, you're actually shown the contents of the inventory.asmx.cs file.

```
using System;
using System.Collections;
using System.ComponentModel;
using System.Data;
using System.Diagnostics;
using System.Web;
using System.Web.Services;

namespace StockWebService
{

    [WebService(Namespace="http://fabrikam.com/XMLWSOrg/")]
    public class XYZ_Inventory : System.Web.Services.WebService
    {
        public XYZ_Inventory()
        {
            //CODEGEN: This call is required by the ASP.NET
            //Web Services Designer
            InitializeComponent();
        }

        //Component Designer generated code
        ⋮
        //
        // Below is the AvailableStock method that returns the
        // quantity of stock onhand.
        //

        [WebMethod]
        public int AvailableStock(string PartNumber)
        {
            return available_inventory(PartNumber);
        }
```

```
//
// The code in the available_inventory procedure would
// probably query a database.
// For this example all the inventory levels are hard-coded!
//
#region available_inventory code
private int available_inventory(string partnumber){
    switch (partnumber){
        case "P00001":
            return 10;
        case "P00002":
            return 13;
        case "P00003":
            return 17;
        case "P00004":
            return 8;
        case "P00005":
            return 0;
        case "P00006":
            return 3;
        case "P00007":
            return 67;
        case "P00008":
            return 34;
        default:
            return 0;


    }
}
#endregion


    }
}
```

Emphasized in the code, somewhere in the middle, is the procedure *AvailableStock*. It takes a single argument of type *string* named *PartNumber* and returns an integer value. *AvailableStock* contains a single line of code that calls the internal function that gets the stock level for the part specified.

On the line prior to *AvailableStock* is the code tag *WebMethod*. You need this tag to inform the compiler that this procedure will be accessed as an operation of a Web service.

Above the class definition line for the *XYZ_Inventory* class is another attribute, *WebService*. You use this attribute to specify the namespace for this Web service. The namespace provides a unique context for the XML body of your Web service. If you left this attribute out, the Web service would default to the namespace *http://tempuri.org/*.

Testing the Web Service

Now press F5 to test the Web service. It's possible to test this Web service without actually writing a client application because ASP.NET Web services provide interfaces based on both HTTP GET and HTTP POST. With .NET version 1.1, the HTTP GET protocol for Web services is disabled by default. HTTP POST is enabled only for requests received from the same machine, which allows you to use a browser to test the Web service if the Web service is on the same machine. You can enable both of these protocols by adding entries in the Web.Config file for the necessary Web service. The following Web.Config file enables the HTTP GET protocol for the Web service:

```xml
<?xml version="1.0" encoding="utf-8" ?>
<configuration>
  <system.web>
    ⋮
    <webServices>
      <protocols>
        <add name="HttpGet" />
      </protocols>
    </webServices>
  </system.web>

  </configuration>
```

With HTTP POST enabled for local requests, you can browse to this Web service and interact with it. Normally, clients use SOAP messages to interact with the Web service, and later you'll want to test this approach, too. For now, using the browser interface is a great productivity benefit.

Figure 1-3 shows the result of entering the Web service URL *http://localhost /XMLWSOrg/Chapter1/StockWebService/Inventory.asmx* into the browser. If you click on AvailableStock, the only operation listed on this Web service, you proceed to a page where you can actually invoke the method. Figure 1-4 shows this page.

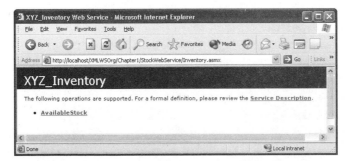

Figure 1-3   Browsing the XYZ_Inventory Web service

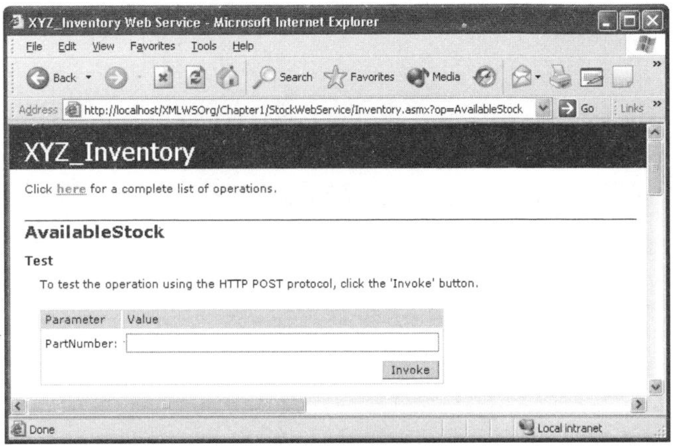

Figure 1-4   The HTTP GET parameter page

If you're actually testing the Web service, as you scroll down this page, ASP.NET provides an example of a SOAP-formatted message and HTTP GET and HTTP POST requests specific to this Web service operation. For now, though, type **P00004** into the PartNumber field and then click the Invoke button. A new browser window is launched, and the results are shown in Figure 1-5. The stock level for P00004 is 8.

Figure 1-5   The resulting XML document from the call to the Web service

Had the code been a little more complex and the process caused an exception, you would have been able to switch to Visual Studio .NET 2003 and debug the Web service.

DISCO and WSDL Documents

DISCO files and WSDL files were discussed earlier in this chapter, but in the creation of the Web service earlier, you didn't construct any of these files. These files were created for you based on the information contained in the project, namely the definition of the class and its methods. You can look at these files by using your browser and entering the appropriate URL.

The DISCO file for your second Web service is *http://localhost/XMLWSOrg /Chapter1/StockWebService/inventory.asmx?DISCO*. The following code shows the result. Notice the single *ContractRef* element in the XML; this element links you to the WSDL file that describes the operation of this Web service.

```
<?xml version="1.0" encoding="utf-8" ?>
  <discovery xmlns:xsd="http://www.w3.org/2001/XMLSchema"
    xmlns:xsi="http://www.w3.org/2001/XMLSchema-instance"
    xmlns="http://schemas.xmlsoap.org/disco/">
    <contractRef ref=
    "http://localhost/XMLWSOrg/Chapter1/StockWebService/inventory.asmx?wsdl"
      docRef=
        "http://localhost/XMLWSOrg/Chapter1/StockWebService/inventory.asmx"
      xmlns="http://schemas.xmlsoap.org/disco/scl/" />
    <soap address=
      "http://localhost/XMLWSOrg/Chapter1/StockWebService/inventory.asmx"
      xmlns:q1=
        "http://fabrikam.com/XMLWSOrg/" binding="q1:XYZ_InventorySoap"
      xmlns="http://schemas.xmlsoap.org/disco/soap/" />
  </discovery>
```

The following WSDL file is returned by replacing DISCO for WSDL in the previous URL:

```
<?xml version="1.0" encoding="utf-8" ?>
  <definitions xmlns:http="http://schemas.xmlsoap.org/wsdl/http/"
    xmlns:soap="http://schemas.xmlsoap.org/wsdl/soap/"
    xmlns:s="http://www.w3.org/2001/XMLSchema"
    xmlns:s0="http://fabrikam.com/XMLWSOrg/"
    xmlns:soapenc="http://schemas.xmlsoap.org/soap/encoding/"
    xmlns:tm="http://microsoft.com/wsdl/mime/textMatching/"
    xmlns:mime="http://schemas.xmlsoap.org/wsdl/mime/"
    targetNamespace="http://fabrikam.com/XMLWSOrg/"
    xmlns="http://schemas.xmlsoap.org/wsdl/">
    <types>
      <s:schema elementFormDefault="qualified"
        targetNamespace="http://fabrikam.com/XMLWSOrg/">
        <s:element name="AvailableStock">
          <s:complexType>
            <s:sequence>
              <s:element minOccurs="0" maxOccurs="1" name="PartNumber"
                type="s:string" />
            </s:sequence>
          </s:complexType>
        </s:element>
        <s:element name="AvailableStockResponse">
          <s:complexType>
```

```
          <s:sequence>
            <s:element minOccurs="1" maxOccurs="1"
              name="AvailableStockResult" type="s:int" />
          </s:sequence>
        </s:complexType>
      </s:element>
    </s:schema>
  </types>
  <message name="AvailableStockSoapIn">
    <part name="parameters" element="s0:AvailableStock" />
  </message>
  <message name="AvailableStockSoapOut">
    <part name="parameters" element="s0:AvailableStockResponse" />
  </message>
  <portType name="XYZ_InventorySoap">
    <operation name="AvailableStock">
      <input message="s0:AvailableStockSoapIn" />
      <output message="s0:AvailableStockSoapOut" />
    </operation>
  </portType>
  <binding name="XYZ_InventorySoap" type="s0:XYZ_InventorySoap">
    <soap:binding transport="http://schemas.xmlsoap.org/soap/http"
      style="document" />
    <operation name="AvailableStock">
      <soap:operation
        soapAction="http://fabrikam.com/XMLWSOrg/AvailableStock"
        style="document" />
      <input>
        <soap:body use="literal" />
      </input>
      <output>
        <soap:body use="literal" />
      </output>
    </operation>
  </binding>
  <service name="XYZ_Inventory">
    <port name="XYZ_InventorySoap" binding="s0:XYZ_InventorySoap">
      <soap:address location=
  "http://localhost/XMLWSOrg/Chapter1/StockWebService/inventory.asmx" />
    </port>
  </service>
</definitions>
```

This file is a little larger than the UTCService WSDL file you looked at earlier. The XML document describes the types, the different message formats supported, and the binding information at the end. One element to look at is the *PartNumber* element, which is inside the *AvailableStock* element in the *Types* element. This information tells someone wanting to access this Web service that a part number can be passed as a string to the Web service.

This simple example shows just how powerful the combination of Visual Studio .NET 2003 and the .NET Framework is for creating Web services. In the chapters to follow, we'll use Web services to provide better solutions to common business problems you face every day. Using the Web service support in .NET, these applications will be efficient and concise.

Extra Credit

The primary goal for this book is to get you thinking about how you can use Web services to solve real problems you face in your business today. To this end, each chapter has an extra credit section that offers you one or more tasks to complete. Some of these tasks involve writing code, and some involve high-level designs either on a given problem or a problem of your own choice. These tasks should help bridge the gap between the artificial solutions presented here and real solutions your business might implement.

Here's your first chance for extra credit. Write a simple Windows Forms application that uses the Web service by utilizing what you've learned in this chapter. Once you've created your form, remember to use the Add Web Reference command to build the proxies for the remote Web service. When you test your application, remember that this client is communicating with the Web service using SOAP. You might also want to use the Trace utility to look at the messages being exchanged.

Summary

In this chapter, you've seen, at a fairly high level, how Web services are accessed and how you can create your own Web services with Visual Studio .NET 2003. You have enough knowledge to be able to create and consume simple Web services. Other issues, such as security, will be covered as you work through the sample applications in later chapters.

2

Supporting Remote Access

Chapters 2 and 3 of this book look at some of the opportunities for XML-based Web services within an organization. This chapter examines the problem of supporting remote staff. It also discusses how to use complex types in Web services. The following chapter looks at using Web services to bridge the gap between your own disparate systems.

Defining the Problem

Many organizations have staff who travel for some portion of their work, as well as employees who work remotely, away from the relative safety of the corporate network. The problem they have is providing the necessary applications to these mobile or remote members of the organization. There are two basic technical approaches to this problem:

- A Web-based application, accessed from a browser by the remote user
- An application running locally on a mobile device

The remote user needs an Internet connection to be able to use the Web-based application. It's not always possible to have an Internet connection available in every business situation. Although a connection to the Internet is available, the application might not lend itself to a browser-based interface, even with the recent advances in browser technology. If a browser based solution is deemed unsuitable, a client-based application might be necessary.

The client-based application, running perhaps on a laptop computer, offers a rich client environment but is isolated from the data stored on the corporate network. It's very likely that the client application will need to work with data from the corporate network and return data to the corporate network. Web services provide a solution to this problem. Web services allow you to send and receive data between the client application and the corporate network. Running Web services over a protocol such as HTTP makes this solution more achievable.

Making the function calls through the Internet between a client and the corporate network is theoretically possible with a number of common protocols such as the Component Object Model (COM) protocol, but in reality, the necessary TCP/IP ports for these protocols are closed on the corporate firewall. A Web service runs over HTTP, whose standard port 80 is more commonly open on corporate firewalls. In a common corporate network security configuration, corporate Web servers and now your XML Web server for supporting these remote applications reside inside a semisecure network behind a first-line firewall. The remainder of the corporate network is within another firewall. This semisecure network segment is often referred to as a *demilitarized zone*, or DMZ. In Chapter 6, you'll see how it's possible to secure the contents of SOAP messages being sent over the Internet.

Applications designed to run on mobile devices are another option for remote access to corporate networks. Today, there are a number of alternatives to the laptop. Personal Digital Assistants (PDAs), smartphones, and Pocket PCs might support a better solution. These devices typically have longer battery life, weigh considerably less, and are more compact than laptops. An example of a company that might want to use an application with a mobile device could be car insurance companies. The companies have customer service representatives who respond to accidents to assist their clients. A Pocket PC is adequate to trap the necessary data at the scene of the accident. Data entered into the Pocket PC can either be held until a wired connection is available, possibly later in the day, or sent over a wireless modem back to a central server. A Web service would be an ideal method of allowing these mobile devices to send their data into the corporate network.

To demonstrate how Web services can be used to support the applications of remote workers, the remainder of this chapter develops a simple Microsoft Word 2002 template and the Web service that provides data to the template.

Developing the Customer Correspondence Template

The sample application you'll develop is based on a Microsoft Word 2002 template. Our fictitious company, Fabrikam, manufactures a range of products that it sells both to other companies and to consumers. The salespeople need to create letters informing their customers about changes in products and pricing. To ensure that the correct contact names and addresses for each company are used, you want to write some functionality into a Word template that will complete the name and address of the customer based on an identity number for that particular company entered by the user. Because letters might be sent to either the CEO or the head buyer at the company, the user needs to be able to specify which contact name is required.

First you create a simple Web service that accepts a company identifier number and returns the name of the company. If you have downloaded and installed this book's sample files, this Web service is already installed for you.

Start Microsoft Visual Studio .NET 2003, and then open the solution from Microsoft Press\XMLWSOrg\Chapter2\FabrikamWebService\FabrikamWebService.sln. This project was created in Visual Studio .NET 2003 by selecting the ASP.NET Web Service template using Microsoft Visual C#. Solution Explorer shows three Web services: SimpleCustomers.asmx, ComplexCustomers.asmx, and OfflineCustomers.asmx. Each will be used at a different point in this chapter. We'll start with a look at SimpleCustomers.asmx.

SimpleCustomers.asmx is a simple Web service, and little code is necessary to create it, as shown here:

```csharp
public class SimpleCustomers : System.Web.Services.WebService
{
    public DataSet fabDataSet;
    public SimpleCustomers()
    {
        InitializeComponent();
        fabDataSet=new DataSet();
        fabDataSet.ReadXml
            ("http://localhost/XMLWSOrg/Chapter2/" & _
                "FabrikamWebService/fabrikam_customers.xml");
    }
    :
    [WebMethod]
    public string CompanyNameFromID(int id) {
        DataRow[] dr;
        dr=fabDataSet.Tables[1].Select("companyid='"+id.ToString()+"'");
        if (dr.Length==0){
            return "Unable to locate the company ID specified";
        }
        else {
            DataRow resultdr=dr[0];
            return resultdr["companyname"].ToString();
        }
    }
}
```

The *CompanyNameFromID* method accepts an integer value and stores it in the variable *id*. An ADO.NET *DataSet* object, referenced by the variable *fabDataSet*, holds a table that contains all the company details. If this were a real application, the *DataSet* would normally be populated using the *Fill* method of a *DataAdapter* object. In this demonstration, *fabDataSet* is loaded with data using the *ReadXml* method of the *DataSet*. This method, as its name suggests, takes an XML file and loads the data contained in it into one or more tables within the *DataSet*.

To get the necessary company name, the *Select* method is called with a filter parameter using the company ID received as an argument. The lines following the *Select* method check to see whether a row in the table matched the company ID and, if so, returns the company name as a string.

Now the server side of this application is complete. The next step is to write the code into the Word 2002 template to use this new Web service.

Using Web Services in an Office Application

Microsoft Office applications have an awesome programming environment available. You can work with Web services from Office XP almost as seamlessly as you can from within Visual Studio .NET 2003 by using the Microsoft Office XP Web Services Toolkit 2. This toolkit adds a tool named the Web Service References Tool into the Office XP development environment that allows you to find Web services using the Universal Description, Discovery, and Integration (UDDI) or Web Services Description Language (WSDL) documents. Once a service is located, the necessary proxy code is generated for you.

The following instructions take you step by step through making a Web service available to any procedure written in a Word 2002 document. The procedure assumes that you have installed Windows Installer 2 (included in Windows XP and Windows 2003 Server) and the Fabrikam Web service from this book's sample files.

1. Download the Microsoft Office XP Web Services Toolkit 2 from this book's sample files (if you haven't already done so).

2. Run the Office XP Web Services Toolkit 2 setup, offwstk.msi.

3. On the Welcome To The Office XP Web Services Toolkit 2.0 Installation Files And Whitepapers Installation page, click Next.

4. On the Readme Information page, click Next.

5. On the Destination Folder page, click Next.

6. On the Ready To Install The Application page, click Next.

7. On the Office XP Web Services Toolkit 2.0 Installation Files And Whitepapers Has Been A Success Page, click Finish.

8. On the Start menu, point to Programs, Office XP Web Services Toolkit 2.0, and click Office Web Services Toolkit Overview to install the Web Service References Tool.

9. Start Word 2002.

10. On the Tools menu, point to Macro and then click Visual Basic Editor.

11. In the Microsoft Visual Basic for Applications (VBA) development environment, click the Tools menu and then click Web Service References.

12. In the Web Service References Tool 2.0 window, click Web Service URL, in the URL box, type **http://localhost/XMLWSOrg/Chapter2 /FabrikamWebService/SimpleCustomers.asmx**, and then click Search, as shown in Figure 2-1.

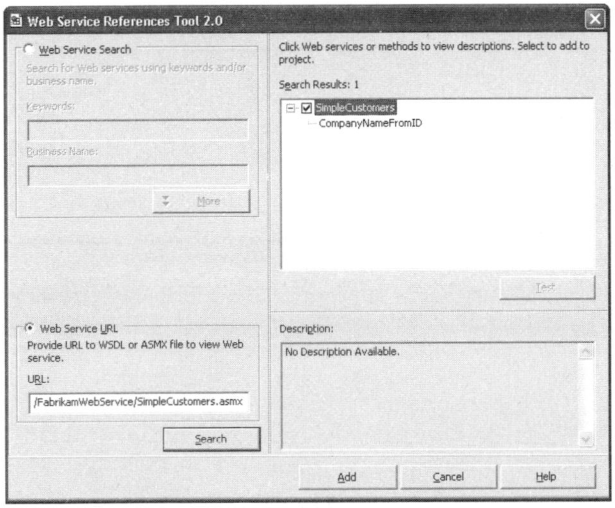

Figure 2-1   The Web Service References Tool 2.0 window

13. Under Search Results: 1, select SimpleCustomers and then click Add.

If you follow the preceding procedure, you'll notice that the Project Explorer window contains a new class module named *clsws_SimpleCustomers*. The code, listed here, is the proxy code generated by the Web Service References Tool:

```
'*******************************************************************
'This class was created by the Web Service References Tool 2.0.
'
'Created: 5/10/2003 07:50:05 AM
'
```

```
'Description:
'This class is a Visual Basic for Applications class representation
' of the Web service
'as defined by http://localhost/XMLWSOrg/Chapter2/FabrikamWebService/
' SimpleCustomers.asmx?wsdl.
'
'To Use:
'Dimension a variable as new clsws_SimpleCustomers, and then write code to
'use the methods provided by the class.
'Example:
' Dim ExampleVar as New clsws_SimpleCustomers
' debug.print ExampleVar.wsm_CompanyNameFromID("Sample Input")
'
'For more information, see Complex Types in Web Service References
'Tool 2.0 Help.
'
'Changes to the code in this class may result in incorrect behavior.
'
'****************************************************************

'Dimensioning private class variables.
Private sc_SimpleCustomers As SoapClient30
Private Const c_WSDL_URL As String = "http://localhost/XMLWSOrg/Chapter2→
/FabrikamWebService/SimpleCustomers.asmx?wsdl"
Private Const c_SERVICE As String = "SimpleCustomers"
Private Const c_PORT As String = "SimpleCustomersSoap"
Private Const c_SERVICE_NAMESPACE As String =
  "http://fabrikam.com/XMLWSOrg"

Private Sub Class_Initialize()
    '****************************************************************
    'This subroutine will be called each time the class is instantiated.
    'Creates sc_ComplexTypes as new SoapClient30, and then
    'initializes sc_ComplexTypes.mssoapinit2 with WSDL file found in
    'http://localhost/XMLWSOrg/Chapter2/FabrikamWebService/
    '  SimpleCustomers.asmx?wsdl.
    '****************************************************************

    Dim str_WSML As String
    str_WSML = ""

    Set sc_SimpleCustomers = New SoapClient30

    sc_SimpleCustomers.MSSoapInit2 c_WSDL_URL, str_WSML, c_SERVICE, _
        c_PORT, c_SERVICE_NAMESPACE
    'Use the proxy server defined in Internet Explorer's LAN settings by
    'setting ProxyServer to <CURRENT_USER>
```

```
      sc_SimpleCustomers.ConnectorProperty("ProxyServer") = "<CURRENT_USER>"
      'Autodetect proxy settings if Internet Explorer is set to autodetect
      'by setting EnableAutoProxy to True
      sc_SimpleCustomers.ConnectorProperty("EnableAutoProxy") = True

End Sub

Private Sub Class_Terminate()
    '*******************************************************************
    'This subroutine will be called each time the class is destructed.
    'Sets sc_ComplexTypes to Nothing.
    '*******************************************************************

    'Error Trap
    On Error GoTo Class_TerminateTrap

    Set sc_SimpleCustomers = Nothing

Exit Sub

Class_TerminateTrap:
    SimpleCustomersErrorHandler ("Class_Terminate")
End Sub

Private Sub SimpleCustomersErrorHandler(str_Function As String)
    '*******************************************************************
    'This subroutine is the class error handler. It can be called
    'from any class subroutine or function
    'when that subroutine or function encounters an error.
    'Then, it will raise the error along with the
    'name of the calling subroutine or function.
    '*******************************************************************

    'SOAP Error
    If sc_SimpleCustomers.FaultCode <> "" Then
        Err.Raise vbObjectError, str_Function, _
            sc_SimpleCustomers.FaultString
    'Non SOAP Error
    Else
        Err.Raise Err.Number, str_Function, Err.Description
    End If

End Sub

Public Function wsm_CompanyNameFromID(ByVal lng_id As Long) As String
    '*******************************************************************
    'Proxy function created from http://localhost/XMLWSOrg/Chapter2/
    '  FabrikamWebService/SimpleCustomers.asmx?wsdl.
```

```
'*****************************************************************

'Error Trap
On Error GoTo wsm_CompanyNameFromIDTrap

wsm_CompanyNameFromID = sc_SimpleCustomers.CompanyNameFromID(lng_id)

Exit Function
wsm_CompanyNameFromIDTrap:
    SimpleCustomersErrorHandler "wsm_CompanyNameFromID"
End Function
```

Most of the processing is handled by a dynamic-link library (DLL) named SOAP30.DLL, which is supplied by the Office XP Web Services Toolkit. This DLL is referenced in the preceding code as

```
Set sc_SimpleCustomers = New SoapClient30
```

The generated code provides a class that bridges between your code and SOAP30.DLL. Your VBA code can now use this class. You should have no need to change any of this code; you simply use the class as it is. Now that the class is set up, you're ready to complete the procedure that will actually add the company name into the Word document.

Using the Generated Class in VBA

To use the class generated by Office XP Web Service Toolkit, you need to add a module file into the VBA development environment. In the Project Explorer window, right-click the name of the project, point to Insert, and then click Module. Add the following code in the Code Editor:

```
Sub Setup_Document()
'
'    First, get the company ID using a simple InputBox.
'
    Dim companyName As String
    Dim companyID As String
    companyID = InputBox("Enter the company ID", _
        "Fabrikam Customer Document")
    If companyID = "" Then Exit Sub
'
'    Now create an instance of the Web service class.
'    This class was generated for you by the Web Service References
'    Tool.
'
    Dim customer_WebService As New clsws_SimpleCustomers
'
'    Use the CompanyNameFromID method passing
```

```
'   the argument of companyID.
'

    companyName = customer_WebService.wsm_CompanyNameFromID(companyID)
End Sub
```

The code creates an instance of the *clsws_SimpleCustomers* class and then calls the *wsm_CompanyNameFromID* method, which passes the company ID obtained by the *InputBox* function. Once this code runs, the company name should be held in the *companyName* variable. To place this data into the Word document, add a bookmark to the location in the document where you want the name to appear and then add the following code to the preceding procedure after the *wsm_CompanyNameFromID* method. (The code assumes that you've named the bookmark *CompanyName*.)

```
Sub Setup_Document()
    ⋮
    companyName = customer_WebService.wsm_CompanyNameFromID(companyID)
'
'   Now set the cursor position in Word to the correct bookmark location
'   and then insert the company name.
'
    Selection.GoTo What:=wdGoToBookmark, Name:="CompanyName"
    Selection.TypeText Text:=companyName
'
'
End Sub
```

The *Setup_Document* procedure is called from the template's *Document_New* procedure, which is called whenever a new document based on the template is created. You can find the Fabrikam.dot template in the Microsoft Press\XMLWSOrg\Chapter2 folder. To run the template, open Word 2002, click File, and then click New. In the New Document task pane, under New From Existing Document, click Choose Document. In the New From Existing Document window, navigate to the folder where you saved the Fabrikam.dot file, click Fabrikam.dot, and then click Create New.

A new document is created based on the Fabrikam.dot template file. You are prompted for a company ID. Enter **1004**, and then click OK. The company name, Coho Vineyard & Winery, is added to the letter. If you aren't prompted for the company ID, your Macro Security settings might be set to High. If you change your Macro Security setting to Medium, you'll be prompted to enable or disable any macros found. (To change your Macro Security setting, point to the Tools menu, point to the Macro submenu, and then click Security.)

You've learned that it's just as easy to access a Web service from within an Office XP application as it is from within a .NET application. However, at this point, your new Word template is not that useful. It only places the name of the company—a single value—into the letter. You really want multiple values—the company name, contact name, and address—inserted into the letter. This problem could be overcome by calling a number of different Web services for each different piece of information required, which would, of course, be very inefficient. A better solution would be to have a single Web service return all the data held about a company in one convenient variable. This variable can't be declared as a simple data type such as string; instead, it is a complex data type. A complex data type contains other data types. It usually organizes simple data types. Your next step is to enhance this existing application by using a complex data type.

Using Complex Data Types

To create a complex data type, return to the Web service and enhance the code a little. If you don't have the Fabrikam Web service open in Visual Studio .NET 2003, open the FabrikamWebService.sln file in the Microsoft Press\XML-WSOrg\Chapter2\FabrikamWebService folder. Now open the ComplexCustomers.asmx file, and display the code.

First you need to create the complex data type that will be returned by the Web service. The following code creates a structure named *CompanyDetails*. This code should be added within the *FabrikamWebService* namespace either before or after the definition of the class *ComplexCustomers*.

```
public struct CompanyDetails{
    public string CompanyName;
    public string CEOName;
    public string BuyerName;
    public string AddressLine1;
    public string AddressLine2;
    public string City;
    public string State;
    public string PostalCode;
    public string TelephoneNumber;
    public string FaxNumber;
    public int CompanyID;
}
```

Now that the structure is defined as a complex data type, the *CompanyName-FromID* method can be renamed to *CompanyDetailsFromID*, and its return type can be set to the new structure *CompanyDetails*, as shown in the following code:

```
public CompanyDetails CompanyDetailsFromID(int companyID) {
    CompanyDetails cd=new CompanyDetails();
    DataRow[] dr;
    dr=fabDS.Tables[1].Select("companyid='"+companyID.ToString()+"'");
```

```
if (dr.Length==0){
    cd.CompanyName="Unable to locate the company ID specified";
    return cd;
}
else {
    DataRow resultdr=dr[0];
    resultdr[0].ToString();
    cd.CompanyName=resultdr["companyname"].ToString();
    cd.AddressLine1=resultdr["addressline1"].ToString();
    cd.AddressLine2=resultdr["addressline2"].ToString();
    cd.City=resultdr["city"].ToString();
    cd.PostalCode=resultdr["postalcode"].ToString();
    cd.State=resultdr["state"].ToString();
    cd.TelephoneNumber=resultdr["telephonenumber"].ToString();
    cd.FaxNumber=resultdr["faxnumber"].ToString();
    cd.CEOName=resultdr["CEO"].ToString();
    cd.BuyerName=resultdr["Buyer"].ToString();
    cd.CompanyID=int.Parse(resultdr["companyid"].ToString());
    return cd;
}
}
```

Other changes in this procedure from the *CompanyNameFromID* proce-dure occur in the first line that creates an instance of the complex data type—the *CompanyDetails* structure—and the code later in the method that actually loads the data from the *DataSet* into the properties of the *CompanyDetails* structure. With these changes, the Web service can return a complex data type that contains multiple values.

Now that the Web service is complete, the client side needs to be updated. If you plan to update the existing template, you should first delete the class file cre-ated for the first Web service, SimpleCustomers.asmx. Next start the Web Service References Tool by clicking the Tools menu and then clicking Web Service Refer-ences in the VBA development environment. Select Web Service URL, and then type the URL **http://localhost/XMLWSOrg/Chapter2/FabrikamWebService /ComplexCustomers.asmx?wsdl**. Notice that in this URL, SimpleCus-tomers.asmx has changed to ComplexCustomers.asmx because this Web service returns the complex data type *CompanyDetails*. Click Search. Under Search Results: 1, select ComplexCustomers and then click Add.

Notice the number of proxy class files generated this time in the Project Explorer window. The class for the Web service is *clsws_ComplexCustomers*. The complex data type is shown as a class named *struct_CompanyDetails*. The final class is *clsof_Factory_ComplexCustom*. This class is used to serialize and deserialize data in COM objects to and from XML in the Web service. Figure 2-2 shows the classes as they are displayed in the Project Explorer window.

Figure 2-2   The proxy classes created by the Web Services References
Tool for the ComplexCustomers Web service

Now that the classes have been changed, the code in the *Setup_Document*
procedure needs to be updated.

```
Sub Setup_Document()
'
'   First, get the company ID and the contact type using InputBox.
'

    Dim companyID As String
    Dim contactType As String

    companyID = InputBox("Enter the company ID", _
        "Fabrikam Customer Visit Document")
    If companyID = "" Then Exit Sub
    contactType = InputBox("Enter contact type to return (CEO or BUYER)", _
        "Fabrikam Customer Visit Document")
'
'   Now create an instance of the Web service class
'   This class was generated for you by the Web Service References
'   Tool.
'

    Dim customer_WebService As New clsws_ComplexCustomers
    Dim companyDetails As struct_CompanyDetails
'
'   Use the CompanyDetailsFromID method passing
'   the argument of CompanyID.
'

    Set companyDetails = _
        customer_WebService.wsm_CompanyDetailsFromID(CompanyID)
'
'   Now set the cursor position in Word to the correct bookmark location
'   and then insert the company name.
'

    Selection.GoTo What:=wdGoToBookmark, Name:="CompanyName"
    If contactType = "CEO" Then
        Selection.TypeText Text:=companyDetails.CEOName
    Else
        Selection.TypeText Text:=companyDetails.BuyerName
```

```
      End If
      Selection.TypeParagraph
      Selection.TypeText Text:=companyDetails.CompanyName
      Selection.TypeParagraph
      Selection.TypeText Text:=companyDetails.AddressLine1
      Selection.TypeParagraph
      Selection.TypeText Text:=companyDetails.AddressLine2
      Selection.TypeParagraph
      Selection.TypeText Text:=companyDetails.City
      Selection.TypeParagraph
      Selection.TypeText Text:=companyDetails.State
      Selection.TypeParagraph
      Selection.TypeText Text:=companyDetails.PostalCode
      Selection.TypeParagraph
    '

    '

End Sub
```

The three statements in this procedure shown in boldface are particularly important. The first statement declares a new instance of the *customer_WebService* class. This instance is needed to actually make the call to the Web service. The second statement declares a variable as type *struct_CompanyDetails*, which is an instance of a class. Finally the third statement, which starts with the VBA *SET* keyword, makes the call to the Web service. Because the *wsm_CompanyDetailsFromID* method returns an object, *SET* is required.

Download the Fabrikam2.dot template from this book's sample files, and use the template to create a Word document to test the new functionality yourself. You'll be prompted to provide the company ID and indicate whether you want the name of the CEO or the chief buyer, and the appropriate details are inserted into the letter.

You will not normally need to look at the actual SOAP messages being sent between the client and server, but because this is the first complex type you have implemented, it's useful to see how complex types are represented in the SOAP message. The following code shows a request message from the client template captured using the Trace Utility from the Microsoft SOAP Toolkit Version 3:

```
<?xml version="1.0" encoding="utf-8"?>
<soap:Envelope xmlns:soap="http://schemas.xmlsoap.org/soap/envelope/"
  xmlns:xsi="http://www.w3.org/2001/XMLSchema-instance"
  xmlns:xsd="http://www.w3.org/2001/XMLSchema">
  <soap:Body>
    <CompanyDetailsFromID xmlns="http://fabrikam.com/XMLWSOrg">
      <companyID>1004</companyID>
    </CompanyDetailsFromID>
  </soap:Body>
</soap:Envelope>
```

The response from the Web service, including the complex type *CompanyDetails*, looks like this:

```xml
<?xml version="1.0" encoding="utf-8"?>
<soap:Envelope xmlns:soap="http://schemas.xmlsoap.org/soap/envelope/"
  xmlns:xsi="http://www.w3.org/2001/XMLSchema-instance"
  xmlns:xsd="http://www.w3.org/2001/XMLSchema">
  <soap:Body>
    <CompanyDetailsFromIDResponse
      xmlns="http://fabrikam.com/XMLWSOrg">
      <CompanyDetailsFromIDResult>
        <CompanyName>Coho Vineyard &amp; Winery</CompanyName>
        <CEOName>Jeanne Bosworth</CEOName>
        <BuyerName>Ryan Calafato</BuyerName>
        <AddressLine1>2030 1St Avenue</AddressLine1>
        <AddressLine2/>
        <City>Paterson</City>
        <State>WA</State>
        <PostalCode>99345</PostalCode>
        <TelephoneNumber>509 555 9812</TelephoneNumber>
        <FaxNumber>509 555 9813</FaxNumber>
        <CompanyID>1004</CompanyID>
      </CompanyDetailsFromIDResult>
    </CompanyDetailsFromIDResponse>
  </soap:Body>
</soap:Envelope>
```

The element that contains the complex type is named *CompanyDetails-FromIDResult*, but if you look at the WSDL document for the Web service by typing **http://localhost/XMLWSOrg/Chapter2/FabrikamWebService /ComplexCustomers.asmx?WSDL** into the browser, you can see that the result is of type *CompanyDetails*.

> **Note**   In Chapter 1, we discussed how to use the Trace Utility to capture SOAP messages. But it isn't easy to capture the preceding message using this utility. The proxy class generated by the Office XP Web Services Toolkit requests the WSDL document for the Web service when the class is instantiated. The class then gets the address of the Web service from the WSDL document. To use the Trace Utility as you did in Chapter 1, you could use this solution to trap the SOAP messages in this chapter: write a simple .NET client application such as a C# Windows application, add the Web service reference to the application, and then hard-code a call to the service with appropriate parameters in a button click event. Make sure to change the URL for the Web service to port 8080, and then start the Trace Utility. Clearly, this solution doesn't test the VBA client code, but it does let you trap the SOAP messages in the Trace Utility.

The Fabrikam customer correspondence template can now return multiple values. After the users provide the required information, the appropriate details are inserted into the letter. However, the solution needs access to the Fabrikam ComplexCustomers Web service. If the user wants to use this template when a network connection is not available, it will fail. The solution can be enhanced by adding offline functionality to it.

Adding Offline Functionality

The remainder of this chapter discusses two approaches to providing an offline capability for the customer correspondence template. The first approach is based on the template and the Web service as developed so far in this chapter. The Web service remains the same, but the code in the template is modified to cache the company details of any companies requested by the user when the Web service can't be reached. The second approach is a more significant modification to the code within both the template and the Web service. This approach uses a client-side cache of all the company details, which are kept in sync with the server-side company details by having the client request updates from a Web service.

Caching the Requested Data on the Client

First let's look at the simpler approach—caching the company details requested by the user on the client. Then we'll discuss the strengths and weaknesses of this approach. The following code creates the *Setup_Document* procedure:

```
Sub Setup_Document()
'
'   First, get the company ID and the contact type using InputBox.
'
    Dim CompanyID As String, contactType As String
    CompanyID = InputBox("Enter the company ID", _
        "Fabrikam Customer Visit Document")
    If companyID = "" Then Exit Sub
    contactType = InputBox("Enter contact type to return (CEO or BUYER)", _
        "Fabrikam Customer Visit Document")
'
'   Now create an instance of the Web service class
'   This class was generated for you by the Web Service References
'   Tool.
'
    Dim customer_WebService As New clsws_ComplexCustomers
    Dim companyDetails As struct_CompanyDetails
'
```

```
'   Use the Get_Company method passing
'   the argument of CompanyID
'
    Set companyDetails = Get_Company(CompanyID)
    If companyDetails Is Nothing Then
        MsgBox "Unable to retrieve information from the Web service" & _
            "or find this record in the local off-line cache!", _
            vbCritical, "Fabrikam"
        Exit Sub
    End If

'
'   Now set the cursor position in Word to the correct bookmark location
'   and then insert the company name.
'
    Selection.GoTo What:=wdGoToBookmark, Name:="CompanyName"
    If contactType = "CEO" Then
        Selection.TypeText Text:=companyDetails.CEOName
    Else
        Selection.TypeText Text:=companyDetails.BuyerName
    End If

    Selection.TypeParagraph
    Selection.TypeText Text:=companyDetails.CompanyName
    Selection.TypeParagraph
    Selection.TypeText Text:=companyDetails.AddressLine1
    Selection.TypeParagraph
    Selection.TypeText Text:=companyDetails.AddressLine2
    Selection.TypeParagraph
    Selection.TypeText Text:=companyDetails.City
    Selection.TypeParagraph
    Selection.TypeText Text:=companyDetails.State
    Selection.TypeParagraph
    Selection.TypeText Text:=companyDetails.PostalCode
    Selection.TypeParagraph
'
'
End Sub
```

The only difference between this code and the previous *Setup_Document* procedure is that the *companyDetails* variable is set with the results of a subroutine named *Get_Company*. Previously, this line called the *wsm_CompanyDetailsFromID* method on the proxy class of the Web service. The *Get_Company* procedure contains the following code:

```
Function Get_Company(CompanyID) As struct_CompanyDetails
    On Error GoTo read_from_cache:
    Dim customer_WebService As New clsws_ComplexCustomers
    Dim offlinecache As DOMDocument
```

```
'
' First open the off-line cache (an XML file).
'
    Set offlinecache = Open_Offline_Cache

    Dim companyDetails As struct_CompanyDetails
'
' Attempt the call to the XML Web Service.
'
    Set companyDetails = _
        customer_WebService.wsm_CompanyDetailsFromID(CompanyID)
'
' As the call was successful, update the local cache with the results.
'
    Update_Offline_Cache offlinecache, companyDetails, CompanyID
'
' Finally return the companyDetails.
'
    Set Get_Company = companyDetails
    Exit Function


read_from_cache:
'
' An error occured!
' Assumption here is that we could not reach the Web service
' and therefore we need to try and get the company details from the
' off-line cache.
'
    Set companyDetails = Get_Cached_CompanyDetails(offlinecache, _
        CompanyID)
'
' And return what we have.
'
    Set Get_Company = companyDetails


End Function
```

Get_Company is the first of a number of procedures that enable the offline functionality of the template. This procedure attempts to call the Web service to get the company details. If the Web service is not available, an error will occur. The error is trapped by the *On Error Goto* statement, and execution is transferred to code that tries to get the company details from the local cache. In this implementation, the local cache is an XML file held on the local machine. Other storage options, such as flat text files or a local database, would also work.

The *Get_Company* procedure makes use of three other procedures. The first, *Open_Offline_Cache*, checks whether the XML file exists and if it does, opens and returns it. If the XML file does not exist, the subroutine creates a new

XML document, adds some structure to it, and saves the file before returning it. The following code creates the *Open_Offline_Cache* procedure:

```
Function Open_Offline_Cache()
Dim XMLDoc As New DOMDocument
'
' First check if the XML document exists.
'
If Dir(ActiveDocument.AttachedTemplate.Path + "\" + _
    "fabrikam_offline.xml") = "" Then
'
' It does not exist, so create it.
'
    Dim root As IXMLDOMNode
    Dim pi As IXMLDOMProcessingInstruction

    Set pi = XMLDoc.createProcessingInstruction("xml", _
        "version=" + Chr(34) + "1.0" + Chr(34))

    XMLDoc.appendChild pi
    Set root = XMLDoc.createNode(NODE_ELEMENT, "CachedCompanyStore", "")
    XMLDoc.appendChild root
'
' Save the new XML Document.
'
    XMLDoc.Save ActiveDocument.AttachedTemplate.Path + "\" + _
        "fabrikam_offline.xml"
Else
'
' The XML document exists, so simply open it.
'
    XMLDoc.Load ActiveDocument.AttachedTemplate.Path + "\" + _
        "fabrikam_offline.xml"
End If
Set Open_Offline_Cache = XMLDoc
End Function
```

The second procedure used in the *Get_Company* procedure is named *Update_Offline_Cache*. As you can see from the following code, this procedure takes the company details received from the call to the Web service and stores them in the offline cache. This procedure creates the XML in the offline cache.

```
Sub Update_Offline_Cache(offlinecache As DOMDocument, _
    companyDetails As struct_CompanyDetails, CompanyID)
Dim node As IXMLDOMNode
'
' Search for the Company record in the XML file by CompanyID.
'
Set node = offlinecache.selectSingleNode _
```

```
        ("//Company[@companyid='" + CompanyID + "']")
If node Is Nothing Then
'
' The company record does not exist in the cache, so add it.
'
    Set node = offlinecache.createNode(NODE_ELEMENT, "Company", "")
    Dim att As IXMLDOMAttribute
    Set att = offlinecache.createAttribute("companyid")
    att.value = CompanyID
    node.Attributes.setNamedItem att
    Add_Element offlinecache, node, "companyname", _
        companyDetails.CompanyName
    Add_Element offlinecache, node, "addressline1", _
        companyDetails.AddressLine1
    Add_Element offlinecache, node, "addressline2", _
        companyDetails.AddressLine2
    Add_Element offlinecache, node, "city", companyDetails.City
    Add_Element offlinecache, node, "postalcode", _
        companyDetails.PostalCode
    Add_Element offlinecache, node, "state", companyDetails.State
    Add_Element offlinecache, node, "telephonenumber", _
        companyDetails.TelephoneNumber
    Add_Element offlinecache, node, "faxnumber", companyDetails.FaxNumber
    Add_Element offlinecache, node, "CEO", companyDetails.CEOName
    Add_Element offlinecache, node, "Buyer", companyDetails.BuyerName
    offlinecache.selectSingleNode("//CachedCompanyStore").appendChild node
Else
'
' The company record does exist in the cache, so update it.
'
    node.selectSingleNode("companyname").Text = _
        companyDetails.CompanyName
    node.selectSingleNode("addressline1").Text = _
        companyDetails.AddressLine1
    node.selectSingleNode("addressline2").Text = _
        companyDetails.AddressLine2
    node.selectSingleNode("city").Text = companyDetails.City
    node.selectSingleNode("postalcode").Text = companyDetails.PostalCode
    node.selectSingleNode("state").Text = companyDetails.State
    node.selectSingleNode("telephonenumber").Text = _
        companyDetails.TelephoneNumber
    node.selectSingleNode("faxnumber").Text = companyDetails.FaxNumber
    node.selectSingleNode("CEO").Text = companyDetails.CEOName
    node.selectSingleNode("Buyer").Text = companyDetails.BuyerName
End If
'
' Save changes to the cache to disk.
'
offlinecache.Save ActiveDocument.AttachedTemplate.Path + "\" + _
    "fabrikam_offline.xml"
End Sub
```

The *Update_Offline_Cache* procedure makes use of another small procedure named *Add_Element*. This procedure is called repeatedly to add specific company details into different elements of the XML document.

```
Sub Add_Element(offlinecache As DOMDocument, node As IXMLDOMNode, _
    elementname As String, value As String)
Dim e As IXMLDOMElement
Set e = offlinecache.createElement(elementname)
e.Text = value
node.appendChild e
End Sub
```

The final procedure of the three used by the *Get_Company* procedure is named *Get_Cached_CompanyDetails*. This procedure builds a *CompanyDetails* instance from the data held in the offline cache, as shown in the following code:

```
Function Get_Cached_CompanyDetails(offlinecache As DOMDocument, _
    CompanyID) As struct_CompanyDetails
Dim companyDetails As New struct_CompanyDetails
Dim node As IXMLDOMNode
'
' Search for the company record in the off-line cache.
'
Set node = offlinecache.selectSingleNode("//Company[@companyid='" + _
    CompanyID + "']")
If Not (node Is Nothing) Then
    companyDetails.CompanyName = node.selectSingleNode("companyname").Text
    companyDetails.AddressLine1 = _
        node.selectSingleNode("addressline1").Text
    companyDetails.AddressLine2 = _
        node.selectSingleNode("addressline2").Text
    companyDetails.City = node.selectSingleNode("city").Text
    companyDetails.PostalCode = node.selectSingleNode("postalcode").Text
    companyDetails.State = node.selectSingleNode("state").Text
    companyDetails.TelephoneNumber = _
        node.selectSingleNode("telephonenumber").Text
    companyDetails.FaxNumber = node.selectSingleNode("faxnumber").Text
    companyDetails.CEOName = node.selectSingleNode("CEO").Text
    companyDetails.BuyerName = node.selectSingleNode("Buyer").Text

    Set Get_Cached_CompanyDetails = companyDetails
End If
End Function
```

This procedure accepts an XML document as the offline cache and an integer as the company identifier. The *selectSingleNode* method is used to return a node of the offline cache that contains the details of the specified company. If the *selectSingleNode* method does not find a matching node, the variable node is set to *Nothing*. The procedure finishes off by setting the properties of the *struct_companyDetails* class instance.

Testing the Offline Functionality

The following procedures take you through a demonstration of the online and offline functionality provided by the template:

1. Start Word 2002.

2. On the File menu, click New.

3. In the New Document task pane, under New From Existing Document, click Choose Document.

4. In the New From Existing Document window, navigate to the folder Microsoft Press\XMLWSOrg\Chapter2. Click the Fabrikam3.dot file, and then click Create New.

5. In the macro warning dialog box, click Enable Macros.

6. At the Company ID prompt, enter **1003** and then click OK.

7. At the CEO or BUYER prompt, enter **CEO** and then click OK.

These steps add the details for City Power and Light to your letter: the name of the CEO, the company name, and the address of the company. Open the folder Microsoft Press\XMLWSOrg\Chapter2. This folder contains the file fabrikam_offline.xml. The following code shows the contents of the XML file at this point:

```
<?xml version="1.0"?>
<CachedCompanyStore>
  <Company companyid="1003">
    <companyname>City Power &amp; Light</companyname>
    <addressline1>Power Plaza</addressline1>
    <addressline2>2nd Floor</addressline2>
    <city>Portland</city>
    <postalcode>97207</postalcode>
    <state>OR</state>
    <telephonenumber>503 555 6723</telephonenumber>
    <faxnumber>503 555 7766</faxnumber>
    <CEO>Bradley Beck</CEO>
    <Buyer>Scott Bishop</Buyer>
  </Company>
</CachedCompanyStore>
```

The previous procedure tests that the template works when the Web service is accessible. The following procedure demonstrates its offline functionality. Being offline is simulated by pausing the Internet Information Services (IIS) Web publishing service on your local server for the duration of the test.

1. Close the document created in the previous procedure.

2. Click Start, and then click Control Panel.

3. In the Control Panel window, click Administrative Tools.

4. In the Administrative Tools window, double-click Services.

5. In the Services window, in the Services (Local) list, click on the World Wide Web Publishing service and then click Pause.

6. Leave the Services window open, and start Word 2002.

7. On the File menu, click New.

8. In the New Document task pane, under New From Existing Document, click Choose Document.

9. In the New From Existing Document window, navigate to Microsoft Press\XMLWSOrg\Chapter2. Click the Fabrikam3.dot file, and then click Create New.

10. In the macro warning dialog box, click Enable Macros.

11. At the Company ID prompt, enter **1003** and then click OK.

12. At the CEO or BUYER prompt, enter **CEO** and then click OK.

13. Click Services in the taskbar.

14. Click Resume to return the World Wide Web Publishing service to normal.

15. Close the Services window.

16. Close the Administrative Tools window.

The name of the CEO of the City Power and Light company and the company's address details are added to the letter, as shown in Figure 2-3. Even though the Web service was not available, the correct details were still returned because these details were obtained from the offline XML cache.

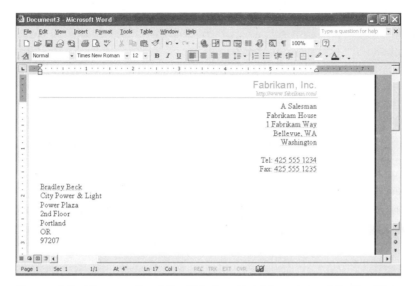

Figure 2-3   The results of the Fabrikam3.dot template while the Web service is disabled

This solution works well for users who are normally online and occasionally offline. If the users have accessed the records they want at least once while they were online, the files will have been added to the offline cache. However, if they had tried to access the company details for company 1006 instead of 1003 while offline, the code would have failed because the details for company 1006 are not stored in the offline cache. If the user will be spending more time offline than online, this solution is not the most efficient, and Web services can be used to develop an alternative approach.

Caching All the Data on the Client

When addressing the needs of users who spend most of their time not connected to the company's main server but who still need to access data and synchronize files, you should consider the second approach—caching all the company details on the client. In this solution, records are always retrieved from a local offline cache, whether the users are online or offline. A separate Web service is used in conjunction with some client code to keep the local offline cache in sync with the records held on the server.

When the customer correspondence template is used for the first time, there's no offline cache. Before attempting to retrieve any company information, the template makes a call to the Fabrikam OfflineCustomers Web service. This call passes one parameter: the current change number held by the client. In this initial state, this change number is 0. The Web service looks to see what records the server holds with a change number higher than the change number submitted by the client. Because the client holds no records in its cache, all the records held by the server are selected to be downloaded to the client. These records are sent to the client, which updates its offline cache and sets its most recent change number to the highest change number against any of the company records received.

Now the offline cache has been populated. The template can retrieve the requested company record from the cache, and the procedure is complete. When the template is used again, the call to the Web service passes the new, higher change number. If no changes to records on the server have occurred, no updated records are returned to the client.

When a record is updated on the server, it's allocated the next sequential change number. When the template makes a subsequent request for updated records, only the updated record is supplied to the local cache.

The advantage to this approach is that apart from the initial download of all the records held on the server, only changed records are downloaded each time the client contacts the server. In the customer correspondence template example, with only several company records, it wouldn't affect the performance of the application to download all the company records and refresh the entire cache every time the template is started. This updated-records-only approach, however, is more useful when the number or size (or both) of the records held on the server increases. If you know your dataset size is small and unlikely to increase, using the updated-records-only solution might be overkill. Understanding your data and its likely changes is critical to effectively designing a synchronizing system such as this one.

Now let's examine each element of this new approach. In this example, the data is stored on the server in an XML file named fabrikam_customers.xml. The XML data looks like this:

```xml
<?xml version="1.0" standalone="yes"?>
<CompanyStore NextSeq="10">
  <Company companyid="1004" UpdateSeq="1">
    <companyname>Coho Vineyard &amp; Winery</companyname>
    <addressline1>2030 1St Avenue</addressline1>
    <addressline2/>
    <city>Paterson</city>
    <postalcode>99345</postalcode>
    <state>WA</state>
    <telephonenumber>509 555 9812</telephonenumber>
    <faxnumber>509 555 9813</faxnumber>
    <CEO>Jeanne Bosworth</CEO>
    <Buyer>Ryan Calafato</Buyer>
```

```xml
</Company>
<Company companyid="1005" UpdateSeq="2">
  <companyname>Contoso, Ltd</companyname>
  <addressline1>Contoso House</addressline1>
  <addressline2>Unit 3, 1334 50th Ave SE</addressline2>
  <city>Everett</city>
  <postalcode>98208</postalcode>
  <state>WA</state>
  <telephonenumber>425 555 3124</telephonenumber>
  <faxnumber>425 555 5222</faxnumber>
  <CEO>Nicole Caron</CEO>
  <Buyer>Pat Coleman</Buyer>
</Company>
<Company companyid="1006" UpdateSeq="3">
  <companyname>Humongous Insurance</companyname>
  <addressline1>5022 3rd Ave South</addressline1>
  <addressline2/>
  <city>Bellingham</city>
  <postalcode>98225</postalcode>
  <state>WA</state>
  <telephonenumber>360 555 9124</telephonenumber>
  <faxnumber>360 555 9882</faxnumber>
  <CEO>Eva Corets</CEO>
  <Buyer>Terry Crayton</Buyer>
</Company>
<Company companyid="1003" UpdateSeq="4">
  <companyname>City Power &amp; Light</companyname>
  <addressline1>Power Plaza</addressline1>
  <addressline2>2nd Floor</addressline2>
  <city>Portland</city>
  <postalcode>97207</postalcode>
  <state>OR</state>
  <telephonenumber>503 555 6723</telephonenumber>
  <faxnumber>503 555 7766</faxnumber>
  <CEO>Bradley Beck</CEO>
  <Buyer>Scott Bishop</Buyer>
</Company>
<Company companyid="1001" UpdateSeq="5">
  <companyname>Adventure Works</companyname>
  <addressline1>Expedition House</addressline1>
  <addressline2>1000 Main Street</addressline2>
  <city>Woodinville</city>
  <postalcode>98178</postalcode>
  <state>WA</state>
  <telephonenumber>425 555 2222</telephonenumber>
  <faxnumber>425 555 3333</faxnumber>
  <CEO>John Arthur</CEO>
  <Buyer>Chris Ashton</Buyer>
</Company>
```

```
<Company companyid="1002" UpdateSeq="6">
  <companyname>Blue Yonder Airlines</companyname>
  <addressline1>1030 Airport Drive</addressline1>
  <addressline2/>
  <city>Renton</city>
  <postalcode>98455</postalcode>
    <state>WA</state>
  <telephonenumber>206 555 2132</telephonenumber>
  <faxnumber>206 555 4332</faxnumber>
  <CEO>Angela Barbariol</CEO>
  <Buyer>Josh Barnhill</Buyer>
</Company>
<Company companyid="1007" UpdateSeq="7">
  <companyname>Lucerne Publishing</companyname>
  <addressline1>The Hexagon</addressline1>
  <addressline2>2544 Rose Street</addressline2>
  <city>San Francisco</city>
  <postalcode>94111</postalcode>
  <state>CA</state>
  <telephonenumber>415 555 6342</telephonenumber>
  <faxnumber>415 555 3227</faxnumber>
  <CEO>Brenda Diaz</CEO>
  <Buyer>Bernard Duerr</Buyer>
</Company>
<Company companyid="1008" UpdateSeq="8">
  <companyname>Northwind Traders</companyname>
  <addressline1>1 Northwind Way</addressline1>
  <addressline2/>
  <city>Denver</city>
  <postalcode>80002</postalcode>
  <state>CO</state>
  <telephonenumber>303 555 6576</telephonenumber>
  <faxnumber>303 555 8345</faxnumber>
  <CEO>Michael Entin</CEO>
  <Buyer>John Frum</Buyer>
</Company>
<Company companyid="1009" UpdateSeq="9">
  <companyname>Proseware, Inc.</companyname>
  <addressline1>102 4th Street</addressline1>
  <addressline2/>
  <city>Bellevue</city>
  <postalcode>98006</postalcode>
  <state>WA</state>
  <telephonenumber>425 555 1222</telephonenumber>
  <faxnumber>425 555 4333</faxnumber>
  <CEO>Chris Gray</CEO>
  <Buyer>Keith Harris</Buyer>
</Company>
</CompanyStore>
```

Notice the *NextSeq* attribute of the *CompanyStore* node that holds the next sequential change number. Also notice that against each *Company* node is an *UpdateSeq* attribute that holds the current change number of each company record.

The Fabrikam OfflineCustomers.asmx file holds the code for the *Get_UpdatedCompanyRecords* method, which sends the updated company records back to the client. Before you look at the method, it's important to examine the *CompanyUpdate* class, as shown here:

```
public class CompanyUpdate{
    public int HighestSeq;
    public int LastSeqSent;
    public CompanyDetails[] UpdatedDetails;
    public CompanyUpdate(){
        UpdatedDetails=new CompanyDetails[5];
    }
}
```

CompanyUpdate is the type that is returned by the Web service. In the previous Web service, ComplexCustomers.asmx, the Web service returned an object of type *CompanyDetails*. In this new Web service, you need to be able to send one or more *CompanyDetails* objects to the client. The *CompanyUpdate* class provides you with the ability to return up to five *CompanyDetails* objects, the highest change number held on the server and the highest change number actually sent within the updated *CompanyDetails* records.

This Web service is designed to send to the client up to five *Company-Details* objects per call to the Web service. If a client requests all the records held on the server, as every client will do at least once, the client doesn't place an extraordinary load on the service. Instead, the client is required to make multiple calls to the server. In this simplified example with only nine company records, this chunking functionality is not necessary, but it's a useful tool for dealing with larger datasets.

The code for the *Get_UpdatedCompanyRecords* procedure is shown here:

```
public CompanyUpdate Get_UpdatedCompanyRecords(int currentseqno) {
    DataSet fabDS=new DataSet();
    fabDS.ReadXml( _
        "http://localhost/XMLWSOrg/Chapter2/" & _
            "FabrikamWebService/fabrikam_customers.xml");
    CompanyUpdate cu = new CompanyUpdate();
    DataRow[] dr;
    int p=0;
    int lastseqsent=0;
    int highestseq=0;
```

```
dr=fabDS.Tables["Company"].Select("","UpdateSeq");
foreach (DataRow r in dr){
    int rowseq=int.Parse(r["UpdateSeq"].ToString());
    if (rowseq>currentseqno && p<5){
        CompanyDetails cd=new CompanyDetails();
        cd.CompanyName=r["companyname"].ToString();
        cd.AddressLine1=r["addressline1"].ToString();
        cd.AddressLine2=r["addressline2"].ToString();
        cd.City=r["city"].ToString();
        cd.PostalCode=r["postalcode"].ToString();
        cd.State=r["state"].ToString();
        cd.TelephoneNumber=r["telephonenumber"].ToString();
        cd.FaxNumber=r["faxnumber"].ToString();
        cd.CEOName=r["CEO"].ToString();
        cd.BuyerName=r["Buyer"].ToString();
        cd.CompanyID=int.Parse(r["companyid"].ToString());
        cu.UpdatedDetails[p]=cd;
        lastseqsent=rowseq;
        p++;
    }
    if (highestseq<rowseq){
        highestseq=rowseq;
    }
}
cu.HighestSeq = highestseq;
cu.LastSeqSent =lastseqsent;
return cu;
}
```

Once the *fabDS* dataset is loaded from the XML file, the records in the Company table are sorted by *UpdateSeq* order using this code:

```
dr=fabDS.Tables["Company"].Select("","UpdateSeq");
```

The *Select* method generates an array of *DataRow* objects, either filtered, sorted, or both. In this case, the code sorts the rows by *UpdateSeq*.

The first five records that have an *UpdateSeq* number greater than the change number (*currentseqno*) passed into the *Get_UpdatedCompanyRecords* method are added into the *UpdatedDetails* array of the *CompanyUpdate* object *cu*. The final job is to set the properties of the *CompanyUpdate* object: *HighestSeq* and *LastSeqSent*. The *HighestSeq* property informs the client of the highest change number, and *LastSeqSent* informs the client of the highest change number passed in this update. If the two numbers are different, the client software should be programmed to make another request until the two numbers match.

The customer correspondence template now needs to be updated to work with the new Fabrikam OfflineCustomers Web service. Your first step is to remove the proxy classes that currently exist in the template that reference ComplexCustomers.asmx.

Delete all the existing class files created for the previous Web service, ComplexCustomers.asmx. Then start the Web Service References Tool by clicking the Tools menu and then clicking Web Service References in the VBA development environment. Select Web Service URL, and then type in the URL as **http://localhost/XMLWSOrg/Chapter2/FabrikamWebService/Offline Customers.asmx?wsdl**. Click Search. Under Search Results: 1, select Offline-Customers and then click Add.

If you have followed along on your machine, you should have a list of classes within your project like the list shown in Figure 2-4. This list is similar to the previous list of proxy classes created by the Web Services References Tool, with the exception of having a new class named *struct_CompanyUpdate*.

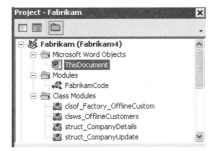

Figure 2-4   The proxy classes created by the Web Service References Tool for the OfflineCustomers Web service

The *Setup_Document* procedure should be amended to look like this:

```
Sub Setup_Document()
'
'   First, get the company ID and the contact type using InputBox.
'
    Dim CompanyID As String, contactType As String
    CompanyID = InputBox("Enter the company ID", _
        "Fabrikam Customer Visit Document")
    contactType = InputBox( _
        "Enter contact type to return (CEO or BUYER)", _
        "Fabrikam Customer Visit Document")
'
'   Now declare and then open the offline cache.
'

    Dim offlinecache As DOMDocument
    Set offlinecache = Open_Offline_Cache

    Update_Cache offlinecache
```

```
    Dim companyDetails As struct_CompanyDetails
    Set companyDetails = Get_Cached_CompanyDetails(offlinecache, _
        CompanyID)

    If companyDetails Is Nothing Then
        MsgBox "Unable to locate details for this company ID!", _
            vbCritical, "Fabrikam"
        Exit Sub
    End If
'
'   Now set the cursor position in Word to the correct bookmark location
'   and then insert the company name.
'
    Selection.GoTo What:=wdGoToBookmark, Name:="CompanyName"
    If contactType = "CEO" Then
        Selection.TypeText Text:=companyDetails.CEOName
    Else
        Selection.TypeText Text:=companyDetails.BuyerName
    End If
    ⋮


'
'

End Sub
```

The majority of the code is the same as that in the previous *Setup_Document* procedure, with several important exceptions, which are shown in boldface. The third statement in boldface makes a call to a procedure named *Update_Cache*, and the fourth retrieves the *companyDetails* object by calling the procedure *Get_Cached_CompanyDetails*. The reason for these changes is that now *CompanyDetails* are always retrieved from the cache, and the first call contains the call to the Web service to get the data to keep the cache up to date. If the call to the Web service fails, the code still expects to get the data it needs from the cache.

The *Get_Cached_CompanyDetails* procedure is the same as it was in the Frabrikam3.dot template. However, you need to create a new procedure to update the cache, as shown in the following code:

```
Sub Update_Cache(offlinecache As DOMDocument)
'
'   Now create an instance of the Web service class.
'   This class was generated for you by the Web Service References
'   Tool.
'
    Dim customer_WebService As New clsws_OfflineCustomers
    Dim companyUpdate As struct_CompanyUpdate
    Dim Updated_CompanyDetails As struct_CompanyDetails
```

```
'
' First get the current SeqNo from the offline cache (XML file).
' This number is passed to the Web service to allow it to work out
' which updates are missing from your offline cache.
'
Dim seqatt As IXMLDOMAttribute
Dim currentseqno, p As Integer
Set seqatt = _
    offlinecache.childNodes(1).Attributes.getNamedItem("SeqNo")
If seqatt Is Nothing Then
    '
    ' If the SeqNo attribute is missing, create it.
    '
    Set seqatt = offlinecache.createAttribute("SeqNo")
    seqatt.value = 0
    currentseqno = 0
    offlinecache.selectSingleNode _
        ("//CachedCompanyStore").Attributes.setNamedItem seqatt
Else
    currentseqno = seqatt.value
End If


'
' Set up the loop to allow for multiple calls to the Web
' service to get the offline cache up to date.
' This is required as the Web service will only send up to five updated
' records at a time.
' This ensures that no single request ties up the service for a
' prolonged period of time.
'
Do

    Set companyUpdate = customer_WebService. _
        wsm_Get_UpdatedCompanyRecords(currentseqno)
    If companyUpdate.LastSeqSent <> 0 Then
        '
        ' Updates received
        ' LastSeqSent is the highest sequence number for the updated
        ' records sent.
        ' If LastSeqSent = HighestSeq, all updates have been
        ' received.
        '
        ' Update the local sequence value with the value LastSeqSent
        ' from the Web service response.
        seqatt.value = companyUpdate.LastSeqSent
        currentseqno = companyUpdate.LastSeqSent

        For p = 0 To 4
```

```
                    Set Updated_CompanyDetails = _
                       companyUpdate.UpdatedDetails(p)
                    If Updated_CompanyDetails.CompanyID <> 0 Then
                        '
                        ' Use the update_offline_cache routine to
                        ' save the updated details.
                        '
                        Update_Offline_Cache offlinecache, _
                           Updated_CompanyDetails, _
                           Updated_CompanyDetails.CompanyID
                    End If
               Next
          End If
     '
     ' Repeat the proceding code until all updates received.
     '
     Loop Until companyUpdate.HighestSeq = companyUpdate.LastSeqSent _
        Or companyUpdate.LastSeqSent = 0


End Sub
```

This procedure is not long; most of the work in updating the cache is done by the *Update_Offline_Cache* procedure. The code in this procedure is there to manage one or more calls to the Web service and to loop through the array of *CompanyDetails* that might be returned.

You can create a Word document based on this new template. Use the Fabrikam4.dot template in the folder Microsoft Press\XMLWSOrg\Chapter2, and test the functionality yourself, as you have done with the other templates. It's worth examining the actual SOAP messages to the OfflineCustomers.asmx Web service so that you can clearly see the repeating *CompanyDetail* elements in the response. In the following example SOAP request, the sequence number passed is 0, indicating that the client has nothing currently cached:

```
<?xml version="1.0" encoding="utf-8"?>
<soap:Envelope xmlns:soap="http://schemas.xmlsoap.org/soap/envelope/"
  xmlns:xsi="http://www.w3.org/2001/XMLSchema-instance"
  xmlns:xsd="http://www.w3.org/2001/XMLSchema">
  <soap:Body>
    <Get_UpdatedCompanyRecords xmlns="http://fabrikam.com/XMLWSOrg">
      <currentseqno>0</currentseqno>
    </Get_UpdatedCompanyRecords>
  </soap:Body>
</soap:Envelope>
```

The SOAP response message looks like this:

```
<?xml version="1.0" encoding="utf-8"?>
<soap:Envelope xmlns:soap="http://schemas.xmlsoap.org/soap/envelope/"
```

```
xmlns:xsi="http://www.w3.org/2001/XMLSchema-instance"
xmlns:xsd="http://www.w3.org/2001/XMLSchema">
<soap:Body>
  <Get_UpdatedCompanyRecordsResponse
    xmlns="http://fabrikam.com/XMLWSOrg">
    <Get_UpdatedCompanyRecordsResult>
      <HighestSeq>9</HighestSeq>
      <LastSeqSent>5</LastSeqSent>
      <UpdatedDetails>
        <CompanyDetails>
          <CompanyName>Coho Vineyard &amp; Winery</CompanyName>
          <CEOName>Jeanne Bosworth</CEOName>
          <BuyerName>Ryan Calafato</BuyerName>
          <AddressLine1>2030 1St Avenue</AddressLine1>
          <AddressLine2/>
          <City>Paterson</City>
          <State>WA</State>
          <PostalCode>99345</PostalCode>
          <TelephoneNumber>509 555 9812</TelephoneNumber>
          <FaxNumber>509 555 9813</FaxNumber>
          <CompanyID>1004</CompanyID>
        </CompanyDetails>
        <CompanyDetails>
          <CompanyName>Contoso, Ltd</CompanyName>
          <CEOName>Nicole Caron</CEOName>
          <BuyerName>Pat Coleman</BuyerName>
          <AddressLine1>Contoso House</AddressLine1>
          <AddressLine2>Unit 3, 1334 50th Ave SE</AddressLine2>
          <City>Everett</City>
          <State>WA</State>
          <PostalCode>98208</PostalCode>
          <TelephoneNumber>425 555 3124</TelephoneNumber>
          <FaxNumber>425 555 5222</FaxNumber>
          <CompanyID>1005</CompanyID>
        </CompanyDetails>
        <CompanyDetails>
          <CompanyName>Humongous Insurance</CompanyName>
          <CEOName>Eva Corets</CEOName>
          <BuyerName>Terry Crayton</BuyerName>
          <AddressLine1>5022 3rd Ave South</AddressLine1>
          <AddressLine2/>
          <City>Bellingham</City>
          <State>WA</State>
          <PostalCode>98225</PostalCode>
          <TelephoneNumber>360 555 9124</TelephoneNumber>
          <FaxNumber>360 555 9882</FaxNumber>
          <CompanyID>1006</CompanyID>
        </CompanyDetails>
```

```xml
<CompanyDetails>
  <CompanyName>City Power &amp; Light</CompanyName>
  <CEOName>Bradley Beck</CEOName>
  <BuyerName>Scott Bishop</BuyerName>
  <AddressLine1>Power Plaza</AddressLine1>
  <AddressLine2>2nd Floor</AddressLine2>
  <City>Portland</City>
  <State>OR</State>
  <PostalCode>97207</PostalCode>
  <TelephoneNumber>503 555 6723</TelephoneNumber>
  <FaxNumber>503 555 7766</FaxNumber>
  <CompanyID>1003</CompanyID>
</CompanyDetails>
<CompanyDetails>
  <CompanyName>Adventure Works</CompanyName>
  <CEOName>John Arthur</CEOName>
  <BuyerName>Chris Ashton</BuyerName>
  <AddressLine1>Expedition House</AddressLine1>
  <AddressLine2>1000 Main Street</AddressLine2>
  <City>Woodinville</City>
  <State>WA</State>
  <PostalCode>98178</PostalCode>
  <TelephoneNumber>425 555 2222</TelephoneNumber>
  <FaxNumber>425 555 3333</FaxNumber>
  <CompanyID>1001</CompanyID>
</CompanyDetails>
        </UpdatedDetails>
      </Get_UpdatedCompanyRecordsResult>
    </Get_UpdatedCompanyRecordsResponse>
  </soap:Body>
</soap:Envelope>
```

Extra Credit

You have two opportunities for extra credit. First is a design task. Consider a real application within your organization that could benefit from offline support. Consider the size of your data, the frequency of changes to the data, and the level of offline support the users of this data need. Consider the advantages and disadvantages of caching only the data that the user accesses when online or caching the entire dataset on the client.

The second task is to step through the Fabrikam4.dot code in the Visual Basic debugger. Add a breakpoint toward the top of *Setup_Document*, and then follow the execution of the code by clicking Step Into on the Debug menu. (The F8 keyboard shortcut is a lot easier.)

Summary

This chapter has accomplished two things. First, it has shown how Web services can be used to support an offline environment, even though some connection to the server must exist at some point. Second, it has introduced the use of complex types within Web services. Without complex types, you must do additional work to return anything more than simple types. The example application in this chapter was basic; however, the techniques used here can be adapted to support many other types of applications. These applications need not be based in an Office XP application; they could be written in other languages or applications.

This chapter also discussed how it's easier to support remote applications with data from the corporate network because Web services run over HTTP. The default HTTP port 80 is often open on firewalls, which allows browsers access to corporate Web sites. That is not to say that port 80 services are not vulnerable to security attacks, but you'll see in Chapter 6 how to secure your Web services.

Integrating Disparate Applications and Systems

Growth by acquisition is a common and relatively quick way for a business to expand. However, for IT departments, successfully integrating the information stores and internal practices of two companies can be a long and sometimes painful process. Even if the plan is eventually to replace the systems in the acquired company with those of the parent, it can take a lot of effort to get the combined company operating productively as soon as possible. Senior management often asks the IT department to integrate data and applications, perhaps running on different platforms, within a short time frame. Integration of such heterogeneous environments, both in the short term and long term, presents the IT professional with pressing responsibilities. XML-based Web services provide an environment and tools equal to the challenge.

This chapter shows you how Web services can make the process of disparate system integration easier. Through the use of XML and a shared transport, Web services provide a common layer of abstraction that allows two systems to communicate. Because both systems can provide and use the Web service, true functional integration, not just data transfer, is possible.

Integrating Systems Using SOAP

Let's begin with an example. You have been tasked with enhancing the product-cost estimating system used by the internal sales staff at Fabrikam. The estimating system currently calculates the cost of a product based on the materials required to meet the customer's product specification. Cost of packaging for the product is set at a default value that doesn't accurately reflect actual cost. Your task is to improve the accuracy of the cost estimate for packaging materials.

You determine that the cost of the packaging materials can be calculated as the price of the packaging material per square meter multiplied by the amount of the packaging material required. However, there's a problem. The estimating system is implemented as a Microsoft Visual Basic .NET application, but the packaging is designed on a UNIX-based computer-aided design package. Your calculation is based on information that must be retrieved from two different platforms.

The Web service solution to this problem is to provide a Web service on the UNIX-based system that accepts a product code and returns the amount of packaging required for the product. The Visual Basic .NET system can then access the Web service on the UNIX system. Because you're accessing functionality rather than data on the UNIX system, the logic or underlying data can change without a need to change the defined interface. You could replace the design package for a newer design package, and as long as the new package implements the same Web service, the estimating system won't need to be updated.

Although Web services solve the basic problems of disparate application integration, other issues still need to be addressed. The data itself will most likely need to be mapped from one system to the other. For example, on one system, the code for Customer A is 1001; on the other system, Customer A is referenced as 3424. You need to map from one code to the other at one end of the connection.

When the number of systems using different customer codes increases, the requirement to map codes from one system to another can become complex. For example, suppose you need to centrally collate the sales figures for a large organization. Each operating unit holds its own sales figures and codes these figures against the customer codes held centrally. You implement a Web service that each operating unit can use to return its sales figures to the central system. The Web service accepts a value for the financial period, the customer code, and the total value of the sales in U.S. dollars. Time passes and your organization acquires 15 new operating units located in Europe and Asia. These operating units sell to some of the same multinational customers that the U.S. operating units sell to, but the customer codes of these acquired systems are different from the codes used in your central database. The problem now is that your Web service expects customer codes that are contained in your central database and financial values in U.S. dollars. Somehow you need to amend the Web service to cater to the data from the foreign operating units without corrupting the definition of the Web service for the existing domestic operating units.

Providing Additional Data with SOAP Headers

One solution to the problem with the Web service just described is to implement a number of additional Web services, perhaps one new service for each operating unit. Each new Web service would map each unit's codes to the central codes and would convert the financial values to U.S. dollars—an obviously inefficient option. Instead, you want to enhance the original Web service in a way that doesn't interfere with how the existing systems use it. As mentioned, the Web service method currently accepts the necessary data: a financial period, a code to represent the customer, and a value for the total sales in that period. For the new operating units, you need to provide a way for them to add some additional data. You would use this additional data to determine which customer code lookup table to use and to identify the currency of the financial values used. If no additional data is provided, you default to the central customer code lookup table and to U.S. dollars. SOAP provides a method for introducing such additional data: SOAP headers.

The SOAP standard requires that any SOAP message consist of a SOAP envelope with a SOAP body inside that envelope. The standard allows for a header element to complement the SOAP body element. SOAP headers provide a mechanism for passing additional information to amend the processing requirements of the existing request or response to the Web service. (A common example of using SOAP headers is to provide user credentials to a Web service. You'll find authentication covered in detail in Chapter 6.) For the sales collating example described previously, you can use SOAP headers to integrate specific information from new units into the central system utilizing the existing Web service. Allow the new operating units to identify themselves as a header in the SOAP request, and use this information to map, if necessary, the customer codes of the remote operating units to the central customer codes. Operating units can also identify the currency in which their figures are reported so that you can convert the values to U.S. dollars before storing them.

You can identify a SOAP header as required or optional. In this example, the header that contains the operating unit code and currency information is optional. If the header file is not present, the Web service assumes that the currency is U.S. dollars and that the customer codes are the standard codes.

In the next section, we'll look at the most basic implementation of SOAP headers. The BasicHeader Web service and the demonstration client application for this section can be downloaded from the sample files that accompany this book.

Creating SOAP Headers

We'll start with a basic Web service and see how to define a SOAP header against a Web method. First you need to create a Web service named Header-Demonstration and create a class that will represent the SOAP header in this

Web service. The following code defines a class named *DemoHeader* that has a single string property named *SourceApplication*:

```
public class DemoHeader:SoapHeader {
    public string SourceApplication;
}
```

The *DemoHeader* class inherits from the *SoapHeader* class, which is a member of the *System.Web.Services.Protocols* namespace. To inherit from *Soap-Header*, you'll need to include the following statement at the top of the file that contains your class:

```
using System.Web.Services.Protocols;
```

The new *DemoHeader* class must inherit from the *SoapHeader* class so that certain properties, such as *DidUnderstand*, are available when a SOAP message is serialized or deserialized to or from an instance of the class. These properties will be covered later in this chapter.

Once the *SoapHeader* class is defined, create a variable to hold an instance of this class, such as in the following code, which is defined within the *HeaderDemonstration* class:

```
public class HeaderDemonstration : System.Web.Services.WebService{
    public DemoHeader myHeader;
    ⋮
}
```

Now that the *myHeader* variable is defined, you can create a Web method that requires the SOAP header to be present. The following code is an example of a simple Web method named *DemoHeaderWebMethod1*:

```
[WebMethod]
[SoapHeader("myHeader")]
public string DemoHeaderWebMethod1() {
    if (myHeader.SourceApplication!=""){
        return "WebMethod1: Source Application "+
            myHeader.SourceApplication ;
    }
    else{
        return "WebMethod1: No source application supplied";
    }
}
```

The second line of the preceding code indicates to the system that a SOAP header is required when this method is called. The structure of the header is taken from the instance of the class held in the *myHeader* variable.

The process is just as straightforward on the client side. When you create the client application and add a Web reference for a Web service that specifies a SOAP header, proxy classes are generated for the Web service and the SOAP header. You create an instance of the header proxy class and then set the necessary properties of the new object. Next you create an instance of the Web service. The last step is to link the header instance to the instance of the Web service, as shown in the following code:

```
private void CallWebMethod1_Click(object sender, System.EventArgs e) {
    localhost.DemoHeader hdr=new localhost.DemoHeader();
    hdr.SourceApplication="ABC";
    localhost.HeaderDemonstration demoWebService=new
        localhost.HeaderDemonstration();
    if (SendHeader1.Checked){
        demoWebService.DemoHeaderValue=hdr;
    }
    MessageBox.Show(demoWebService.DemoHeaderWebMethod1());
}
```

The Web service proxy class contains a property named *<header-name>Value*. In the preceding code, the property for *DemoHeader* is *Demo-HeaderValue*. The *SendHeader1* variable references the *CheckBox* control on the form of the demonstration application. The *CheckBox* control allows you to decide whether you want to send the SOAP header when the Web service method is called.

If you have downloaded the Web service and demonstration client application for this chapter, you can run this Web method by following these instructions:

1.   Start the DemoHeaderClient application in Visual Studio .NET 2003.

2.   In the Header Demo window, under Test WebMethod1, select the Send Header check box and then click Call WebMethod1.

3.   A message box will appear stating "WebMethod1: Source Application ABC."

If you try this procedure again without checking the check box to send the SOAP header, you'll get a *SoapException* error. The additional information in the error states that the object reference isn't set to an instance of an object. This error occurs when the Web service expects a SOAP header and you don't provide one. *WebMethod1* demands at least one SOAP header conforming to its definition as contained in the Web service's Web Services Description Language (WSDL) document. Although you really don't need to concern yourself with the SOAP message, it's interesting to see the header in the message using the Microsoft SOAP Toolkit Version 3 Trace Utility:

```
<?xml version="1.0" encoding="utf-8" ?>
<soap:Envelope xmlns:soap="http://schemas.xmlsoap.org/soap/envelope/"
```

```
xmlns:xsi="http://www.w3.org/2001/XMLSchema-instance"
xmlns:xsd="http://www.w3.org/2001/XMLSchema">
<soap:Header>
  <DemoHeader xmlns="http://fabrikam.com/XMLWSOrg">
    <SourceApplication>ABC</SourceApplication>
  </DemoHeader>
</soap:Header>
<soap:Body>
  <DemoHeaderWebMethod1 xmlns="http://fabrikam.com/XMLWSOrg" />
</soap:Body>
</soap:Envelope>
```

In the sales collating example earlier in this chapter, the SOAP header was optional. You make a SOAP header optional by setting the *Required* parameter to *false* in the *SoapHeader* attribute. The following code for *WebMethod2* in the HeaderDemonstration Web service makes the SOAP header optional:

```
[WebMethod]
[SoapHeader("myHeader",Required=false)]
public string DemoHeaderWebMethod2() {
    if (myHeader != null && myHeader.SourceApplication=="ABC" ){
        return "WebMethod2: Source Application "+
            myHeader.SourceApplication ;
    }
    else{
        return "WebMethod2: No source application supplied";
    }
}
```

Run the DemoHeaderClient application, and test it again. Call *WebMethod1* without sending the SOAP header, and you'll receive a *Soap-Exception* error. You can call *WebMethod2* with or without a SOAP header. If you call *WebMethod2* without a SOAP header, a message box will appear stating "WebMethod2: No source application supplied."

Providing Transaction Functionality with SOAP Headers

When integrating different systems, it's not always possible to package all the data required to perform some action into a single request. You must break the data across a number of calls to a Web service but have these calls treated as if they happened at once. In other words, you create the concept of a single logical transaction across one or more calls to a Web service. For example, you might be able to modify or enhance a legacy system to be a client of a Web service, but it might be necessary, or just simpler, to bind different elements of data into a single transaction within the Web service rather than in the legacy application.

> **Note**   ASP.NET supports a useful tool called *automatic transactions*. A transaction is a group of related actions that can normally be committed as a single operation. By setting the *Transaction* property of the *WebMethod* attribute to *TransactionOption.RequiresNew*, any interactions with resource managers such as Microsoft SQL Server or Microsoft Message Queue Server (MSMQ) are contained within a transaction. All actions within the transaction are committed only if no errors occur during the call to the Web method. Apart from setting the property, no further action is required on your part. However, transactions in this chapter do not refer to this feature. This section discusses how to build your own custom transactions using *SoapHeader* attributes.

To demonstrate how these transactions operate, we'll work through the code of the Fabrikam Orders Web service and a client application that interacts with it. You open the solution for the Web service from Microsoft Press\XMLWSOrg \Chapter3\FabrikamWebService2\FabrikamWebService2.sln and the Fabrikam test application at Microsoft Press\XMLWSOrg\Chapter3\Fabrikam-TestApplication\FabrikamTestApplication.sln.

Examining the Fabrikam Orders Web Service

The Fabrikam Orders Web service provides methods that allow other applications to add order information into an XML file held on the Web server. To keep the focus on the transaction functionality within the Web service, the functionality in this example has deliberately been kept simple. The following code shows the XML file structure:

```
<Orders NextOrderNumber="2">
  <Order Number="1" Customer="134">
    <Items>
      <Item ItemNumber="12" Qty="3" />
      <Item ItemNumber="13" Qty="2" />
    </Items>
  </Order>
</Orders>
```

Rather than support a single method that adds an order and its associated items, this Web service supports the following methods:

■ *AddOrder(int customer, bool StartTransaction)*

■ *AddItem(int order, int itemnumber, int quantity)*

■ *CommitTransaction(int transaction)*

The *AddOrder* method accepts a numeric customer number and a Boolean value indicating whether a transaction should be started. The *AddOrder* method returns the next sequential order number. If the *StartTransaction* argument is *true*, a new transaction is created and its reference number is returned in a SOAP header. With the returned order number, use the *AddItem* method to add items to the order. *AddItem* requires a valid order number, a numeric item number, and an integer value for the quantity of the items to add to the order. The *CommitTransaction* method is used to make the changes permanent and to close the transaction.

Implementing the *AddOrder* method

The following code creates the *AddOrder* method in the Fabrikam Orders Web service. Much of the code is used to manipulate the XML data file.

```
[WebMethod]
[SoapHeader("transHeader",Required=false,
           Direction=SoapHeaderDirection.Out)]
public int AddOrder(int customer,bool StartTransaction)
{
    Application.Lock();
    XmlDocument xmld=(XmlDocument)Application["OrdersXML"];
    tm=(TransactionManager)Application["TransactionManager"];
    if (tm==null){
        tm=new TransactionManager();
    }
    XmlNode nextordernumbernode= xmld.ChildNodes[0].Attributes.
        GetNamedItem("NextOrderNumber","");
    int nextordernumber=int.Parse(nextordernumbernode.Value);

    XmlNode rootnode=xmld.SelectSingleNode("Orders");
    XmlNode ordernode=xmld.CreateNode(XmlNodeType.Element,"Order","");
    XmlNode attnode=xmld.CreateNode(XmlNodeType.Attribute,"Number","");
    attnode.Value = nextordernumber.ToString();

    int UpdateNextOrderNumber=nextordernumber+1;
    nextordernumbernode.Value=UpdateNextOrderNumber.ToString();

    ordernode.Attributes.SetNamedItem(attnode);
    attnode=xmld.CreateNode(XmlNodeType.Attribute,"Customer","");
    attnode.Value =customer.ToString();
    ordernode.Attributes.SetNamedItem(attnode);
    rootnode.AppendChild(ordernode);

    Application["OrdersXML"]=xmld;
    if (StartTransaction){
```

```
        transHeader=new TransactionHeader();
        transHeader.Transaction=this.StartTransaction();
    }
    Application["TransactionManager"]=tm;
    Application.UnLock();
    return nextordernumber;
}
```

The second and third lines of code, which appear in boldface, contain a lot of information. First, the *SoapHeader* attribute is based on the contents of the *transHeader* variable. By setting the *Required* property to *false*, *SoapHeader* is optional. Second, the *Direction* property indicates that this *SoapHeader* will be sent from the server to the client. The *Direction* property of the *SoapHeader* attribute can be set to *SoapHeaderDirection.In*, *SoapHeaderDirection.Out*, or *SoapHeaderDirection.InOut*. This is the first example of an outbound SOAP header in this chapter.

The use of *Application.Lock* and *Application.Unlock* are important within this procedure. In this contrived example, the XML data file is held with ASP.NET using the *Application* object. The *Lock* and *Unlock* methods ensure that only a single client is able to access the contents of the *Application* object. You probably wouldn't use this approach in the real world because it would not scale if the number of concurrent clients grew. While the *Application* object is locked, other requests are blocked until the lock is cleared. A solution that would not have these scaling problems would be based around a database, such as SQL Server, using row-level locking. You can then allow multiple active users while ensuring data integrity.

If the *StartTransaction* variable is *true*, the code creates an instance of the *TransactionHeader* class. The variable that holds this reference must be the same as the one referenced in the *SoapHeader* attribute. After the instance is created, the *StartTransaction* method is called and returns the next available transaction reference.

Implementing the *AddItem* method

The *AddItem* method shown in the following code either adds an item to an order or caches the instruction. The code caches the instruction if a valid transaction number is passed in the SOAP header.

```
[WebMethod]
[SoapHeader("transHeader",Required=false,
        Direction=SoapHeaderDirection.In)]
public int AddItem(int order,int itemnumber,int quantity){
    Application.Lock();
```

```
TransactionManager tm=(.TransactionManager)
    Application["TransactionManager"];
if (transHeader!=null){
    if (tm.validtransaction(transHeader.Transaction)){
        cached_item_call c=new cached_item_call();
        c.itemnumber=itemnumber;
        c.order=order;
        c.qty=quantity;
        tm.Add_Transaction(c,transHeader.Transaction);
        Application["TransactionManager"]=tm;
        Application.UnLock();
        return -1;
    }
    else {
        SoapException se = new
            SoapException("Transaction not found!",
                SoapException.ClientFaultCode);
        Application.UnLock();
        throw se;
    }
}
else {
    XmlDocument xmld=(XmlDocument)Application["OrdersXML"];
    XmlNode ordernode=xmld.
        SelectSingleNode("//Order[@Number="+order.ToString()+"]");
    if (ordernode==null){
        SoapException se = new
            SoapException("Order not found!",
                SoapException.ClientFaultCode);
        Application.UnLock();
        throw se;
    }
    else {
        XmlNode itemsnode=ordernode.SelectSingleNode("Items");
        if (itemsnode==null){
            itemsnode=xmld.
                CreateNode(XmlNodeType.Element,"Items","");
            ordernode.AppendChild(itemsnode);
        }
        XmlNode itemnode=xmld.
            CreateNode(XmlNodeType.Element,"Item","");
        XmlNode attnode=xmld.
            CreateNode(XmlNodeType.Attribute,"ItemNumber","");
        attnode.Value = itemnumber.ToString();
        itemnode.Attributes.SetNamedItem(attnode);
        attnode=xmld.CreateNode(XmlNodeType.Attribute,"Qty","");
        attnode.Value =quantity.ToString();
        itemnode.Attributes.SetNamedItem(attnode);
```

```
        itemsnode.AppendChild(itemnode);
        Application["OrdersXML"]=xmld;
        Application.UnLock();
        return -1;
    }
  }
}
```

Let's look first at the *SoapHeader* attribute and its properties. You can read from this code that

■ A SOAP header can be deserialized into the *transHeader* object.

■ This SOAP header is not required.

■ This SOAP header is expected on the SOAP request message, that is to say, inbound to the Web service.

If a transaction header is passed with the SOAP request, the procedure first validates that the transaction number passed is actually a live transaction. This check is accomplished by calling the *ValidateTransaction* method of the *TransactionManager* class. If the transaction is not located, the code will notify the client application that an error occurred by creating an instance of the *SoapException* class and using the *Throw* statement.

The *SoapException* constructor method allows you to set details of the *SoapException* instance created. Two parameters are supplied to the constructor in the preceding code. The first parameter sets the message of the *Soap-Exception*. The second parameter provides the client with information about where the fault lies. For example, the error is marked as being a client fault (*SoapException.ClientFaultCode*) because the transaction sent from the client can't be found. If the Web service was unable to process the SOAP request because a necessary resource for the Web service was not available, a server fault (*SoapException.ServerFaultCode*) would be thrown. A client receiving a server fault exception might send the SOAP message again later because the SOAP message itself was not at fault.

Implementing the *CommitTransaction* Method

The *CommitTransaction* method shown in the following code doesn't use any SOAP header information because the transaction number is passed as an argument of the method itself. Because the method deals only with transactions, it's sensible to make the transaction number an argument. If the transaction is valid, the cached instructions for the transaction are executed.

```
[WebMethod]
public int CommitTransaction(int transaction){
```

```
Application.Lock();
tm=(TransactionManager)Application["TransactionManager"];
if (!tm.validtransaction(transHeader.Transaction)){
    SoapException se = new SoapException(
        "Transaction not found!",SoapException.ClientFaultCode);
    Application.UnLock();
    throw se;
}
else{
    Queue q=tm.Return_Transaction_Queue(transaction);
    cached_item_call c;
    while (q.Count>0) {
        c=(cached_item_call)q.Dequeue();
        if (c!=null){
            AddItem(c.order,c.itemnumber,c.qty);
        }
    }
    Application.UnLock();
    return -1;
}
}
```

Using Transaction Support from the Client

Now that the code for the Web service is complete, you can see how a client interacts with the Fabrikam Orders Web service. The client will call the *AddOrder* method once, the *AddItem* method one or more times, and finally the *CommitTransaction* method. Calling the *AddOrder* method from the client needs little code, as shown here:

```
localhost.Orders ordersWebService=new localhost.Orders();
int orderNumber=ordersWebService.AddOrder(100,true);
int transactionNumber=0;
if (ordersWebService.TransactionHeaderValue!=null){
    transactionNumber=ordersWebService.
        TransactionHeaderValue.Transaction;
}
```

In this code, a new order is created against customer 100 and a request is made to start a new transaction. The SOAP header from the Web service is deserialized into a *TransactionHeader* object and can be referenced from the *TransactionHeaderValue* property of the Web service instance.

Calling the *AddItem* method is straightforward, as shown in the following code. An instruction to add item 333 to order 10 for a quantity of 5 is added to the transaction number held in the *transactionNumber* variable. The value held in the *transactionNumber* variable would have been returned from an earlier call to the *AddOrder* method. Another instruction is then cached to add item 444 to order 10 for a quantity of 2. Finally the *CommitTransaction* method is called.

```
localhost.TransactionHeader transHeader=new localhost.TransactionHeader();
transHeader.Transaction=transactionNumber;
localhost.Orders ordersWebService=new localhost.Orders();
ordersWebService.TransactionHeaderValue=transHeader;
ordersWebService.AddItem(10,333,5);
ordersWebService.AddItem(10,444,2);
ordersWebService.CommitTransaction(transactionNumber);
```

Because of the headers involved, it isn't possible to test the Web service from the HTTP GET browser–based interfaces provided by ASP.NET. If you have downloaded and examined the code for the Fabrikam Orders Web service, you've noticed two additional Web methods that I haven't mentioned in this chapter. These methods, *ShowOrdersXML* and *OpenTransactions*, are used by the test application to show you the open transactions and the state of the Fabrikam_Orders.xml file held on the server. To test the Web service, follow the steps in the next procedure. The test application has two windows. One window displays the Fabrikam_Orders.xml file as it is held on the server and the other provides a user interface to the three Web methods discussed earlier (*AddOrder*, *AddItem*, and *CommitTransaction*). See Figure 3-1.

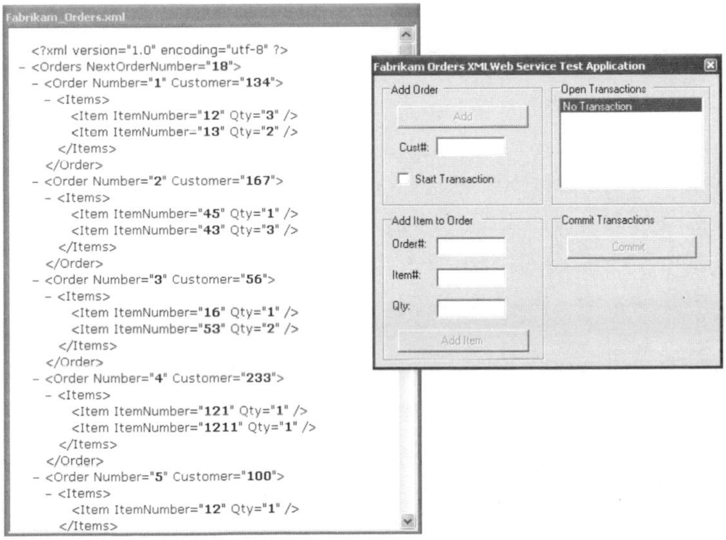

Figure 3-1   The FabrikamWebService2 test application

1. Open and run the solution located at Microsoft Press\XMLWS-Org\Chapter3\FabrikamTestApplication\FabrikamTestApplication.sln in Visual Studio .NET 2003.

2. In the Fabrikam Orders XML Web Service Test Application window, under Add Order, in the Cust# field, type **100** and then click Add. A new order is created immediately in the XML file.

3. Click OK to close the message box.

4. Under Add Item To Order, in the Order# field, enter the order number reported in step 2.

5. In the Item# field, enter **777** as the item number.

6. In the Qty field, enter **10** and then click Add Item. The line item is added to the order immediately.

7. Click OK to close the message box.

8. Under Add Order, in the Cust# field, type **200**, select Start Transaction, and then click Add. The new order is created immediately, and a new transaction is opened.

9. Click OK to close the message box.

10. Under Add Item To Order, in the Order# field, enter the order number reported in step 8.

11. In the Item# field, enter **888** as the item number.

12. In the Qty field, enter **5**.

13. In the list of Open Transactions, click the transaction added to the list when you created the new order.

14. Now click Add Item. The item does not appear in the Fabrikam_Orders.xml file. The instruction is cached on the server.

15. Click OK to close the message box.

16. In the list of Open Transactions, click the active transaction number and then click Commit. The cached instructions are processed and the items appear in the XML file.

17. Click OK to close the message box.

As this Web service currently stands, you can cache an instruction to add an item to any order in the XML file, not just to the order against which the transaction was initiated. You could, of course, add the necessary code to validate the order against the transaction.

Understanding Header Properties

I mentioned earlier in the chapter that inheriting from the *SoapHeader* class provides certain properties to your header class, such as *Actor*, *MustUnderstand*, and *DidUnderstand*. The *Actor* property allows you to set the Uniform Resource Identifier (URI) of the intended recipient of the header. SOAP allows for a SOAP message to be passed to its final destination through a number of intermediate "hops." By using the *Actor* property, you can identify the contents of the header as being destined for a particular hop along the route to the destination.

Suppose a company implements a Web service that accepts SOAP messages that are actually destined for other Web services. The purpose of this new Web service is to give mobile client applications with intermittent connections to the Internet the ability to hand off SOAP messages to this Web service, which then attempts to forward the SOAP messages to their final destination. If the final destination is not available, the intermediate Web service can periodically repeat the request. Results from calls to the final destination Web service can be held by the intermediate service until the client requests these messages. Client applications can add a header to their SOAP request that's destined for the intermediate Web service to specify how long the service should attempt to send the SOAP message to its final destination. Obviously, this model works only for SOAP messages in which the client doesn't need an immediate response.

The *MustUnderstand* and *DidUnderstand* properties are related to the *MustUnderstand* attribute of the SOAP header element. *MustUnderstand* in a SOAP header is set to *true* or *false*. (*1* or *0* is also allowed.) It's possible that a client might send your Web service a header element in a SOAP message that your Web service did not specify. According to the SOAP specification, if the header is not marked with a *MustUnderstand* attribute or if it's set to *MustUnderstand="false"* (or *MustUnderstand="0"*), your Web service is allowed to ignore the header. However, if the header is marked *MustUnderstand="true"* (or *MustUnderstand="1"*), your Web service must process the information in the header. To inform ASP.NET that your code handles a particular header, set the *DidUnderstand* property to *true*. For headers that your Web service doesn't understand, set the *DidUnderstand* property to *false* for each header you process. (ASP.NET makes the assumption that you do process the headers marked with *MustUnderstand="true"*.)

Extra Credit

Here's your extra credit opportunity for this chapter. Consider the following proposed Web service, and decide what information should be carried in the body of the SOAP message.

Your Human Resources (HR) department wants to make some personnel information available in Microsoft Excel to the company's managers. You plan to integrate the HR application with Excel using a Web service. The HR department requires that everyone be able to access non-confidential data on any employee, such as the department the employee works in. Only the employee's manager will be allowed to access confidential information such as salary data. The Web service inputs must include an employee number, and they might require a user identification and the password of a manager. How would you design this Web service? Consider what, if anything, should be carried in the SOAP body and SOAP header sections of the SOAP message.

The confidential information returned by the Web service should be encrypted to secure the data while it's transferred between the service and the client. You can find out how to encrypt a Web service in Chapter 6.

Summary

This chapter started with a discussion of the challenges involved in integrating disparate systems and applications and how Web services can help meet those challenges. Interoperability is achieved by providing a platform that's common to many systems. That platform uses SOAP messages held as XML and a ubiquitous transport mechanism to pass these messages in the form of HTTP.

The remainder of the chapter discussed using SOAP headers to provide additional information about the SOAP message. Only the SOAP envelope and body elements are required in a SOAP message; SOAP headers are optional. Proxy code deserializes a SOAP header into an object that you can handle in your code. Although SOAP headers aren't called for in all Web services, they're another valuable tool developers can call on when the situation warrants them.

4

Developing Electronic Business-to-Business Communication

To be successful, a business must be able to communicate with its subsidiaries, partners, and customers in an efficient, accurate, and timely manner. Even a small business in today's highly technical business environment works with vast amounts of information, far more than the traditional secretary and bookkeeper can manage. Automation isn't an option—it's a necessity.

However, automating your company's communication system is only the first step. You must also find a way for your system to connect with the systems of your partners and customers. They have just as many choices in architectures, platforms, and software as you do, and there's no guarantee that you'll all settle on similar or even compatible approaches. XML-based Web services offer the greatest possibilities for establishing productive business-to-business communication.

Understanding Electronic Data Interchange

Establishing business-to-business communication is by no means new; organizations have been exchanging business messages with their trading partners electronically since the 1960s. Because no standards existed then, the more powerful partner in the relationship generally dictated the message structure and format that the other partner would have to work with. By late in the decade, standards began to emerge, and electronic data interchange (EDI) was born.

EDI is the electronic replacement of paper documentation. Although an EDI message can be created and sent in a format specific to a trading partner, messages are more commonly formatted to a particular standard. The advantage of using standards is that if your trading partner already supports that message format, little if any additional programming is required for it to work with your message. To get past the problems of different architectures and platforms, EDI messages are usually created as flat text files with either fixed-length fields or character-delimited fields. Although EDI usage has grown considerably since the late 1960s, it has not grown as significantly as many analysts of that time thought it would. Not unlike paper communication, EDI has some problems of its own.

Making Sense of the Standards

Many groups define EDI message standards. For example, in the United States, the American National Standards Institute (ANSI) has a range of EDI messages referred to as ANSI X12. Numerous industries have developed their own EDI standards. The Public Warehousing Industry created the Warehousing Industry Network Standards (WINS); the retail and grocery industry created standard purchase order and invoice messages. The European car industry established a non-profit organization for developing business-to-business communication called ODETTE. (See *http://www.odette.org* for more information.) The United Nations is responsible for an EDI standard called the Electronic Data Interchange for Administration, Commerce, and Transport—usually abbreviated to UN/EDIFACT. Many organizations are now standardizing on the use of EDI-FACT messages.

If you work with trading partners in different industries, you'll likely have to support EDI messages from different standards bodies. Even within standards set by one group, a message type, such as a purchase order, might have a number of versions.

In addition, as the needs of companies have evolved, so have the structure of the EDI messages that support them. To ensure communication between partners as message formats change, most EDI messages detail within the message version information to uniquely identify the structure used to create the message. As a result, the messages themselves can be quite daunting. To make them intelligible to as many entities as possible, the messages have to contain hundreds of fields of information—some optional, but many required.

Looking at a Sample Order Response Message

The following example shows the complexity of a simple order response message in an EDI format, and many common EDI messages are considerably longer than this one. The message is an EDIFACT order response (ORDRSP) message version D96A that simply acknowledges that a single order was accepted as is. This message would be more complicated if the order was accepted with amendments.

Message Data	Description
`UNA:+.? '`	Service string advice (code UNA) details the delimiters used in the message
`UNB+UNOA:3+SUPPLIERCODE:QUAL+` `CUSTOMERCODE:QUAL+021204:2100` `+12345'`	Interchange header (code UNB) starts and identifies an interchange
`UNG+ORDRSP+SENDERIDENTITY:QUAL` `+RECIPIENTIDENTITY:QUAL+` `021204:2100+0001+UN+` `D:96A:EAN005'`	Functional group header (code UNG) specifies from and to information
`UNH+1+ORDRSP:D:96A:UN:EAN005'`	Message header (code UNH) details the message version used
`BGM+231+ORDERNUMBER+29'`	Beginning of message (code BGM); 29 is code to indicate that the order was accepted without amendment
`DTM+137:20021204:102'`	Date and time (code DTM) of message (137) 12/4/2002
`DTM+2:200212052200:203'`	Date and time of requested delivery (2) 12/5/2002 at 22:00
`NAD+ST+SHIPTOLOCATIONCODED::92'`	Name and address (code NAD) of ship to (ST) location as an agreed code
`NAD+SU+87654321::92'`	Name and address of supplier's location (SU) as an agreed code
`UNS+S'`	Section control (code UNS)
`MOA+86:100.00'`	Monetary amount (code MOA) of this message 100.00
`CNT+1:162'` `CNT+2:0'`	Control total (code CNT) to enable the receiver to cross check the message
`UNT+12+1'`	Message trailer (code UNT)
`UNE+1+0001'`	Functional group trailer (code UNE) includes count of function groups 1
`UNZ+1+12345'`	Interchange trailer (code UNZ) includes interchange reference 12345

Many companies, especially smaller ones, have avoided EDI because of cost. Although it's possible to write custom software to parse EDI messages, and packages are available that interface between your computer systems and the EDI messages of your trading partners, both options are expensive. Also, until fairly recently, EDI messages were sent to and from trading partners through a value-added network (VAN). VANs act as an intermediate storage facility between partners and typically charge by the number of messages or the volume of data sent. Either way, this operation is a considerable expense.

The Internet is changing the way companies exchange EDI messages. You can now exchange EDI messages using a number of Internet protocols, such as FTP or SMTP, which makes the transaction less expensive than working through a VAN.

Another recent technical innovation to impact EDI is XML. A number of organizations now develop standard XML schemas for common messages such as invoices and purchase orders. The obvious advantage of XML over flat text files is that you don't need an expensive parser to manipulate and work with the data. (Microsoft Internet Explorer ships with an XML parser.)

Choosing Between EDI and Web Services

EDI is no longer the only option for enabling business-to-business communication. Because Web services are platform- and architecture-independent, they lend themselves to addressing this business need. The following questions can help you decide if using EDI or a Web service is best for your organization:

- What is the state of EDI adoption within your industry?

- Can your application accept the typical latency involved in EDI-based communication?

- How many of your customers and suppliers support EDI messages?

If your competitors are using EDI, you should consider whether they are developing a competitive advantage by doing so. Also, there's little point in investing time and energy implementing EDI for one partner if you can't benefit from that effort with others. If you have a partner anxious to use EDI but feel it's the exception rather than the rule, you should consider converting that partner to Web services.

EDI is typically a message-based, store-and-forward system and might have inherent latency problems that aren't acceptable to you. Web services offer a more tightly coupled integration between your partners' systems and your own. For example, your company provides a credit reporting service, and your partner wants to take telephone inquiries from its customers and immediately accept or reject a customer's application for a line of credit. A Web service would allow your partner to integrate your credit-reporting data into its systems quickly enough to make decisions while the customer is still on the phone. A message-based EDI system can't pass information quickly enough to meet that requirement.

Designing a Business-to-Business Connection with Web Services

Once you've decided that Web services are the way to go, you and your partner must decide on the specific requirements of a system that addresses everyone's needs. The following topics can guide that discussion:

- **Agree on the purpose of the information exchange.** For example, you need to send and receive purchase order information or to share delivery forecasts.

- **Agree on the type of data that needs to be exchanged.** For example, a purchase order message needs to include order number, part number, quantity, delivery location, and delivery time.

- **Agree on the mapping of any existing codes.** For example, your company refers to your remote manufacturing site as 002 and your partner refers to this location as 52.

- **Agree on an appropriate level of security.** If you're exchanging a delivery forecast, you and your trading partner might agree that encrypting these messages isn't necessary. For messages about finances, however, security is a major concern and encryption—of all elements—is essential.

- **Agree on the exceptions that each Web service can raise.** If a purchase order references an order that already exists (and is not an amendment), should the Web service return a particular value or throw a suitable exception?

- **Agree on a testing strategy.** The strategy might be as simple as hosting the Web service on two servers, one for test and one for the live environment. You might agree to include a parameter used as a flag on each Web service that indicates whether the call should be treated as test data or live data.

The remainder of this chapter explores two example Web services for exchanging a delivery forecast with a trading partner. As you'll see, there are also choices for the format of the data passed over the Web service.

Implementing the Delivery Forecast System Using an Object-Based Approach

If you've downloaded this book's sample files, you can open the solution for this Web service in Microsoft Visual Studio .NET 2003. The path to the solution is Microsoft Press\XMLWSOrg\Chapter4\ObjectBased\ObjectBased.sln. The Web service itself is contained in the file Delfor.asmx. The Web service supports two methods, *ClearForecast* and *CreateForecast*.

The *ClearForecast* method is defined as

```
public System.Boolean ClearForecast (System.String partnumber)
```

This method is used by your trading partner to clear the forecast for the specified part number. The Web service stores the forecast information in a Microsoft Access database. In a production Web service, you should expect to use a database capable of scaling, such as Microsoft SQL Server.

The code behind the *ClearForecast* method looks like this:

```
[WebMethod]
public bool ClearForecast(string partnumber) {
    try{
        oleDbDataAdapter1.Fill(partForecast1);
        for(int rp=partForecast1.Forecast.Rows.Count;rp>0;rp--){
            partForecast.ForecastRow fr=(partForecast.ForecastRow)
                partForecast1.Forecast.Rows[rp-1];
            if (fr.PartID.ToString()==partnumber){
                fr.Delete();
            }
        }
        oleDbDataAdapter1.Update(partForecast1);
        return true;
    }
    catch{
        return false;
    }
}
```

The *oleDbDataAdapter1* variable references an ADO.NET *DataAdapter* object that the code uses to retrieve the contents of the Forecast table held in the Access database Forecast.mdb. The *Fill* method of the *DataAdapter* class places the data into the *DataSet* object *partForecast1*. The next block of code iterates through the rows in the *DataSet* and marks those rows whose part number matches that specified in the call to the method for deletion. Finally the *Update* method of the *DataAdapter* is called to persist the changes in the actual database table. Notice that the method returns *true* if no errors occur and *false* if an error is trapped. This method could have been written to raise a *SoapException* instead.

The *CreateForecast* method is defined as

```
public System.Boolean CreateForecast( System.String partnumber,
    ObjectBased.ForecastItem[] forecastitems,
    System.Boolean clearforecast)
```

Your trading partner will use this method to supply a delivery forecast for a particular part number. The method accepts a part number, an array of forecast items, and the Boolean value *clearforecast*. The *ForecastItem* type is a complex type that consists of a date and a quantity. Let's examine the code for this method.

```
[WebMethod]
public bool CreateForecast(string partnumber,ForecastItem[]
    forecastitems,bool clearforecast) {
    oleDbDataAdapter2.Fill(dsParts1);
    bool found=false;
    foreach(dsParts.PartsRow r in dsParts1.Parts){
        if( r.ID.ToString()==partnumber){
            found=true;
        }
    }
    if(found){
        if(clearforecast){
            ClearForecast(partnumber);
        }
        try{
            oleDbDataAdapter1.Fill(partForecast1);

            foreach(ForecastItem f in forecastitems){
                partForecast.ForecastRow r=
                    partForecast1.Forecast.NewForecastRow();
                r.PartID=partnumber;
                r.Date =f.date;
                r.Quantity =(int)f.quantity;
                partForecast1.Forecast.AddForecastRow(r);
            }
            oleDbDataAdapter1.Update(partForecast1);
            return true;
        }
        catch{
```

```
            return false;
        }
    }
    else{
        return false;
    }
}
```

The first seven lines of the method are used to check that the part number specified in the method is a valid part. The *DataAdapter* object *oleDbDataAdapter2* retrieves the contents of the Parts table and loads the contents into the *DataSet* object *dsParts1*.

If the part number is found, the procedure checks to see whether the value of the *clearforecast* variable is *true*. If the value is *true*, the *ClearForecast* method is called to clear the forecast for the part number specified.

Finally *oleDbDataAdapter1* is used to populate the *DataSet* object *partForecast1* from the Forecast table. A *foreach* structure is used to loop through the *forecastitems* array. A new row is added to the dataset for each forecast item. Once all items have been processed, the *Update* method of the *DataAdapter* object is called to persist the forecast back to the Forecast table in the database. As in the *ClearForecast* method, the *Update* method returns *true* if successful and *false* if an error occurs.

Testing the Object-Based Forecast Solution

In Visual Studio .NET 2003, open the solution file Microsoft Press\XMLWS-Org\Chapter4\ObjectBasedClient\ObjectBasedClient.sln. This is a simple Microsoft Windows application that provides a user interface to the Web service.

The following steps allow you to test the solution:

1. In Visual Studio .NET 2003, click Start on the Debug menu.

2. In the Part Code box, type **A0000045**.

3. In the Quantity field, type **10** and then click Add.

4. In the Date field, add 1 to today's date.

5. Change the quantity to **25**, and then click Add.

6. Add 2 to today's date.

7. Change the quantity to **5**, and then click Add. (The client should look like Figure 4-1 at this stage, although your dates will be different.)

8. Click Send.

9. Click OK to close the Forecast Successfully Uploaded message box.

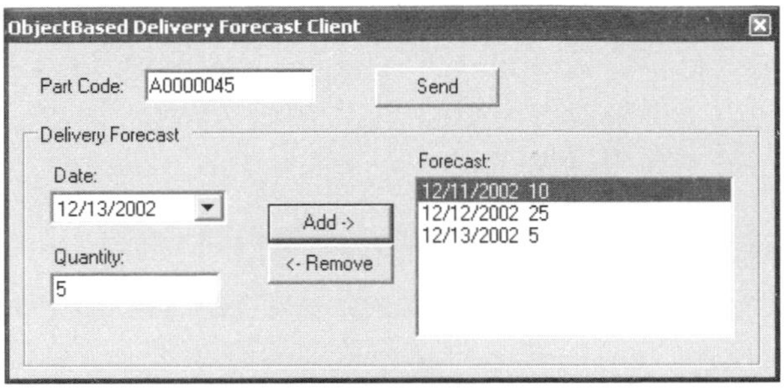

Figure 4-1   The object-based client before sending the forecast

To make it a little easier to view the forecast held in the Access database on the server, I've included an ASP.NET Web page that displays the contents of the Forecast table. Open Internet Explorer, and enter **http://localhost/XMLWSOrg /Chapter4/ObjectBased/ForecastDisplay.aspx**.This object-based solution to passing a delivery forecast certainly works. However, having the data received as an object requires you to do some additional programming to store the data in the database. An alternative design for this problem is to keep the data as XML. You can still use a Web service as the transport, but you can leverage some of the XML support found in other parts of the Microsoft Windows .NET Framework to make it easier to store the data.

Implementing the Delivery Forecast System Using an XML-Based Approach

The second example Web service we'll look at in this section solves the same delivery forecast problem but works a little differently from the previous forecast Web service. In this approach, your trading partner can send the forecast for multiple parts, with multiple dates and quantities, in a single call to your Web service. This solution takes advantage of the XML support built into the *DataSet* object (contained in the *System.Data* namespace). The *DataSet* object supports the *ReadXml* method. This Web service solution uses the overloaded *ReadXml* method that accepts a path to a file. *ReadXml* will read the data contained in this XML file into the *DataSet* object. The Web service is implemented to receive a string of data that is actually an XML document. The Web service then saves the XML document temporarily to the file system so that the *ReadXml* method of the *DataSet* object can load the data. Finally an *oleDbDataAdapter* is used to persist the data from the *DataSet* into the Forecast table of the Access database. The definition of the Web method is

```
public System.Boolean CreateForecast (System.String xmlstr)
```

As in the object-based Web service solution, the *CreateForecast* method returns a Boolean value to indicate whether the method was successful. The method accepts a single parameter, the string *xmlstr*. The following code generates the *CreateForecast* method:

```
[WebMethod]
public bool CreateForecast(string xmlstr)
{
    //
    // Place the XML string into a StringReader object.
    //
    StringReader strReader=new StringReader(xmlstr);
    //
    // Create an XmlTextReader object from the StringReader object.
    //
    XmlTextReader xmlTextReader=new XmlTextReader(strReader);
    //
    // Clear the Forecast table.
    //
    OleDbCommand command=new OleDbCommand(
        "DELETE * from Forecast",oleDbConnection1);
    oleDbConnection1.Open();
    command.ExecuteNonQuery();
    oleDbConnection1.Close();

    DataSet ds=new DataSet();
    //
    // Load the DataSet from the XmlTextReader.
    //
    ds.ReadXml(xmlTextReader);
    oleDbDataAdapter1.Update(ds);
    return true;
}
```

First a *StringReader* object is created using the string passed to the Web service. The *StringReader* class is an implementation of the abstract *TextReader* class and is used to read characters from a string. The next line of code creates an *XmlTextReader* from the *StringReader* object. The next block of code clears the Forecast table, getting it ready to accept the new forecast. Finally the *DataSet* object is loaded from the *XmlTextReader* object, and the *Update* method is called on the *oleDbDataAdapter1* object to persist the changes in the database table.

Testing the XML-Based Forecast Solution

In Visual Studio .NET 2003, open the solution file Microsoft Press\XMLWS-Org\Chapter4\XMLBasedClient\XMLBasedClient.sln. As with the object-based test client, this application provides a simple client to the XML-based Web service. This test client looks a little different because you can specify the forecast for more than one part at a time. The following instructions show how to test the XML-based delivery forecast solution:

1. In Visual Studio .NET, click Start on the Debug menu.

2. In the Quantity box, type **100** and then click Add.

3. In the Date field, add 1 to today's date.

4. In the Quantity box, type **250** and then click Add.

5. Change the Part Code to **B0000102**.

6. In the Quantity box, type **178** and then click Add.

7. In the Date field, add 2 to today's date.

8. In the Quantity box, type **93** and then click Add. (The client should look similar to Figure 4-2, although your dates will be different.)

9. Click Send to pass the forecast to the Web service.

10. Click OK to close the Forecast Successfully Uploaded message box.

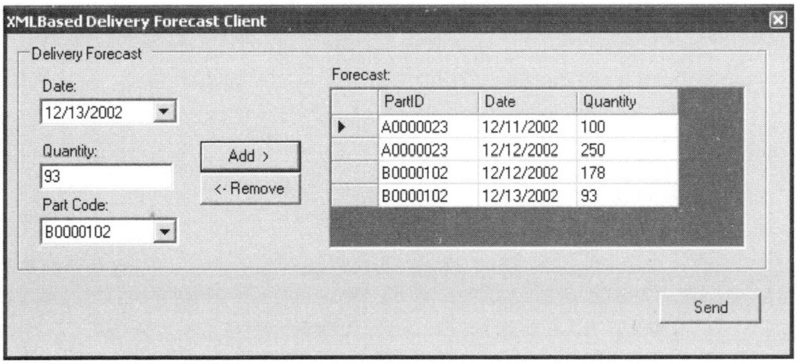

Figure 4-2   The XML-based client before sending the forecast

Again, as with the object-based Web service, you can display the contents of the Forecast table held in the Access database by entering **http://localhost /XMLWSOrg/Chapter4/XMLBased/ForecastDisplay.aspx** in your browser.

Comparing the SOAP Messages

Both the object-based Web service and the XML-based Web service achieve the same goal, although they work with the data differently in the SOAP message. The following SOAP request, trapped using the Microsoft SOAP Toolkit Version 3 Trace Utility (see Chapter 1), was generated by the object-based Web service:

```xml
<?xml version="1.0" encoding="utf-8"?>
<soap:Envelope xmlns:soap="http://schemas.xmlsoap.org/soap/envelope/"
  xmlns:xsi="http://www.w3.org/2001/XMLSchema-instance"
  xmlns:xsd="http://www.w3.org/2001/XMLSchema">
  <soap:Body>
    <CreateForecast xmlns="http://fabrikam.com/XMLWSOrg">
      <partnumber>
        A0000045
      </partnumber>
      <forecastitems>
        <ForecastItem>
          <date>
            2002-12-11T00:00:00.0000000-08:00
          </date>
          <quantity>
            10
          </quantity>
        </ForecastItem>
        <ForecastItem>
          <date>
            2002-12-12T00:00:00.0000000-08:00
          </date>
          <quantity>
            25
          </quantity>
        </ForecastItem>
        <ForecastItem>
          <date>
            2002-12-13T00:00:00.0000000-08:00
          </date>
          <quantity>
            5
          </quantity>
        </ForecastItem>
      </forecastitems>
      <clearforecast>
        true
      </clearforecast>
    </CreateForecast>
  </soap:Body>
</soap:Envelope>
```

By now, you should be familiar with the structure of this SOAP message. The SOAP body consists of well-formed XML that contains the part number and a number of *ForecastItem* elements, each of which contains a date and quantity element. Compare the object-based request to the XML-based SOAP request shown here:

```xml
<?xml version="1.0" encoding="utf-8"?>
<soap:Envelope xmlns:soap="http://schemas.xmlsoap.org/soap/envelope/"
  xmlns:xsi="http://www.w3.org/2001/XMLSchema-instance"
  xmlns:xsd="http://www.w3.org/2001/XMLSchema">
  <soap:Body>
    <CreateForecast xmlns="http://fabrikam.com/XMLWSOrg">
      <xmlstr>
        <NewDataSet>
          <Forecast>
            <PartID>A0000023</PartID>
            <Date>2002-12-11T00:00:00.0000000-08:00</Date>
            <Quantity>100</Quantity>
          </Forecast>
          <Forecast>
            <PartID>A0000023</PartID>
            <Date>2002-12-12T00:00:00.0000000-08:00</Date>
            <Quantity>250</Quantity>
          </Forecast>
          <Forecast>
            <PartID>B0000102</PartID>
            <Date>2002-12-12T00:00:00.0000000-08:00</Date>
            <Quantity>178</Quantity>
          </Forecast>
          <Forecast>
            <PartID>B0000102</PartID>
            <Date>2002-12-13T00:00:00.0000000-08:00</Date>
            <Quantity>93</Quantity>
          </Forecast></NewDataSet>
      </xmlstr>
    </CreateForecast>
  </soap:Body>
</soap:Envelope>
```

As you can see, the XML data passed as a string is coded to ensure that the string data doesn't corrupt the SOAP message. This string is decoded before it's processed by your code in the Web service.

The XML-based solution requires less code because it leverages the XML awareness of the *DataSet* object, but one problem remains. When your trading partner examines the Web Services Description Language (WSDL) file of the object-based Web service, it's apparent from the WSDL file which data needs to be passed. In the XML-based solution, the WSDL file is different, as shown in the following code:

```xml
<?xml version="1.0" encoding="utf-8"?>
<definitions xmlns:http="http://schemas.xmlsoap.org/wsdl/http/"
  xmlns:soap="http://schemas.xmlsoap.org/wsdl/soap/"
  xmlns:s="http://www.w3.org/2001/XMLSchema"
  xmlns:s0="http://fabrikam.com/XMLWSOrg"
  xmlns:soapenc="http://schemas.xmlsoap.org/soap/encoding/"
  xmlns:tm="http://microsoft.com/wsdl/mime/textMatching/"
  xmlns:mime="http://schemas.xmlsoap.org/wsdl/mime/"
  targetNamespace="http://fabrikam.com/XMLWSOrg"
    xmlns="http://schemas.xmlsoap.org/wsdl/">
<types>
  <s:schema elementFormDefault="qualified"
    targetNamespace="http://fabrikam.com/XMLWSOrg">
    <s:element name="CreateForecast">
      <s:complexType>
        <s:sequence>
          <s:element minOccurs="0" maxOccurs="1" name="xmlstr"
            type="s:string" />
        </s:sequence>
      </s:complexType>
    </s:element>
    <s:element name="CreateForecastResponse">
      <s:complexType>
        <s:sequence>
          <s:element minOccurs="1" maxOccurs="1"
            name="CreateForecastResult" type="s:boolean" />
        </s:sequence>
      </s:complexType>
    </s:element>
    <s:element name="boolean" type="s:boolean" />
  </s:schema>
</types>
<message name="CreateForecastSoapIn">
  <part name="parameters" element="s0:CreateForecast" />
</message>
<message name="CreateForecastSoapOut">
  <part name="parameters" element="s0:CreateForecastResponse" />
</message>
<portType name="DELFORSoap">
  <operation name="CreateForecast">
    <input message="s0:CreateForecastSoapIn" />
    <output message="s0:CreateForecastSoapOut" />
  </operation>
</portType>
<binding name="DELFORSoap" type="s0:DELFORSoap">
```

```
    <soap:binding transport="http://schemas.xmlsoap.org/soap/http"
      style="document" />
    <operation name="CreateForecast">
      <soap:operation soapAction=
        "http://fabrikam.com/XMLWSOrg/CreateForecast" style="document" />
      <input>
        <soap:body use="literal" />
      </input>
      <output>
        <soap:body use="literal" />
      </output>
    </operation>
  </binding>
  <service name="DELFOR">
    <port name="DELFORSoap" binding="s0:DELFORSoap">
      <soap:address location=
        "http://localhost/XMLWSOrg/Chapter4/XMLBased/DELFOR.asmx" />
    </port>
  </service>
</definitions>
```

The boldface lines define the *xmlstr* parameter as a string. Although using a string is entirely accurate because the Web service expects a string, it doesn't inform your partner what data the string should contain. You can get around this problem by sending your partner an XML schema document such as the following:

```
<?xml version="1.0" standalone="yes"?>
<xs:schema id="NewDataSet" xmlns=""
  xmlns:xs="http://www.w3.org/2001/XMLSchema"
  xmlns:msdata="urn:schemas-microsoft-com:xml-msdata">
  <xs:element name="NewDataSet" msdata:IsDataSet="true">
    <xs:complexType>
      <xs:choice maxOccurs="unbounded">
        <xs:element name="Forecast">
          <xs:complexType>
            <xs:sequence>
              <xs:element name="PartID" type="xs:string" minOccurs="0" />
              <xs:element name="Date" type="xs:dateTime" minOccurs="0" />
              <xs:element name="Quantity" type="xs:int" minOccurs="0" />
            </xs:sequence>
          </xs:complexType>
        </xs:element>
      </xs:choice>
    </xs:complexType>
  </xs:element>
</xs:schema>
```

There are various ways of generating this schema; you can write it yourself or use tools such as Visual Studio .NET. This schema was generated from the following code:

```
DataSet forecast=new DataSet();
DataTable forecastTable=forecast.Tables.Add("Forecast");
DataColumn PartIDCol=forecastTable.Columns.Add("PartID",typeof(string));
DataColumn DateCol=forecastTable.Columns.Add
    ("Date",typeof(System.DateTime));
DataColumn QuantityCol=forecastTable.Columns.Add("Quantity",typeof(int));
forecast.WriteXmlSchema
    (@"C:Microsoft Press\XMLWSOrg\Chapter4\forecast.xsd");
```

First you create a new *DataSet* object referenced by a variable named *forecast*. This object is empty, so the next task is to create a table within it. The four boldface lines create the columns of the table: PartID, Date, and Quantity. Finally the *DataSet* object's *WriteXmlSchema* method creates the schema and writes it to the file specified.

Extra Credit

First design a Web service that your trading partner can use to send you an order. Consider what data you need to receive and what you will do with the information. Second write code that creates two tables in a single *DataSet* object and persists the schema to a file. Inspect the schema file to see how the two tables are detailed. For double credit, define a relationship between the two tables and see how the schema changes.

Summary

EDI is a valid way to communicate with your business partners and customers, but it isn't particularly easy to use. This chapter showed how Web services can be used instead of traditional EDI and how Web services provide tighter integration with less latency. The other new concept in this chapter was using XML data passed as a string instead of passing serialized objects. In the XML-based Web service solution, the XML was used to load a *DataSet* object.

This chapter made a quick mention of security in business-to-business communication. Chapter 6 explores security further by discussing how to authenticate that a request originated from your trading partner and how to encrypt the data.

Connecting with Customers

This chapter focuses on connecting with customers. You might not directly deal with your customers; other companies might do so for you. But whether the relationship is direct or not, it's important to support your customers and maintain that relationship.

First we'll examine indirect customer relationships. Although another company deals with your customers for you, you still might want to provide these customers with support. Customer support can also be a great way to promote related products or services, and examples of this type of service can be found on the Internet. For example, delivery companies receive a significant amount of business by shipping products from a Web site where the customer bought a product. Indirectly, the customer has paid for delivery of the item. Often, customers can track the progress of their parcels using the delivery company's Web site. Sometimes, but not always, they can track the parcels from the site where they actually purchased the items.

You might be thinking that having users track orders through the delivery company is not really a problem. After all, most users are happy to browse to the site of the delivery company to check the status of their parcels. However, not all indirectly linked companies are so well known. The customers have placed their orders with you, so they should be able to come back to you to check on the status of their orders, including any services provided by a third party.

There are many different approaches to integrating third-party data into your own Web site, including:

- **Branding.** Branding is simple but reasonably effective. The third party supplying the particular service creates a Web page matching the look and feel of your Web site. You provide your customers a link from your site to this branded page. This linkage can also be accomplished using an HTML frame, a technique that hides the URL from the customer. The disadvantage of a branded page is that you really have lost control of the page and, effectively, your customer as well.

■ **Data replication.** A little more complicated, data replication involves the third-party company supplying to you the necessary data that you can then present to your user. Clearly, this data needs to be kept up to date, perhaps by updating it on a nightly basis. The disadvantage of this approach is the need to replicate the data.

■ **Custom data integration.** Even more complicated, custom data integration involves accessing the data on the third party's servers from your own servers, possibly using a transport protocol such as HTTP. Of course, you could use other protocols such as COM or low-level packet protocols such as TCP. The disadvantage with these protocols, of course, is the requirement to allow packets to pass through any network firewalls. If you use a custom HTTP-based protocol, the disadvantage is the time and money you expend developing this solution. Each company you choose to partner with might need its own custom solution.

This is not a complete list, but it's enough to highlight the different approaches that can be taken and some of their disadvantages. Hopefully, seeing the mention of HTTP as a transport made you think of XML-based Web services as a possible solution to this problem.

Using Web Services to Support Customers

What you really want is to have pages on your Web site that access and present the data the user needs, whether that data is from your own business objects or from the business objects of your partners. Using Web services to access this data allows you to integrate with functionality on remote servers no matter what that platform is.

In the previous chapters, we have started each time by creating the Web service and then creating the client-side proxy based on the Web Services Description Language (WSDL) file from the Web service. Although this approach is the most common, clients of the Web service might need to define the interface they expect on the remote Web service. Let's look at how to define Web service interfaces.

Defining a Web Service Interface to Be Implemented by Others

The sample application for this chapter contains a few pages of the Satellite Installation Web site. These pages allow customers of the Web site to enter their personal details, select a satellite system that they want installed, and then check for an available installation appointment. For now, assume that you're technically responsible for this Web site. Your company does not actually have installation engineers of its own; instead, you contract out this part of your service to many different installation companies throughout the country. You want the service your customers receive to be quick and efficient. You need to tightly integrate your Web site to the systems of all the different installation companies. You decide to use Web services because being platform-agnostic is definitely a necessity of this solution. But even though you're going to be a client of many remote Web services, you define the interfaces they should support, which makes integrating with each remote Web service very simple. In fact, all you need to do is keep a list of each Web service's URL.

You inform each partner company (the installation providers) what interfaces they need to support by sending them a WSDL file. We've covered WSDL files previously, so they shouldn't be new to you. You could write the WSDL file manually, but in this case, it's easier to create the Web service interfaces in Microsoft Visual Studio .NET 2003 yourself and then query the service for the WSDL file. You do not need to implement each method; just define what the method should look like. For example, for the Satellite Installation company, you want the remote Web services to support three interfaces: *GetAppointment*, *ConfirmAppointment*, and *CancelAppointment*, as shown in the following code:

```
namespace InstallCompany2 {

    [WebService(Namespace="http://fabrikam.com/XMLWSOrg")]
    public class Install : System.Web.Services.WebService {

        public Install() {
        :
        [WebMethod]
        public AppointmentInfo GetAppointment(customerinfo cust,
            string ordertype){
            return null;
        }

        [WebMethod]
        public bool ConfirmAppointment(string custref,string orderref) {
            return true;
        }
```

```
    [WebMethod]
    public bool CancelAppointment(string custref,string orderref){
        return true;
    }
}
public class customerinfo{
    public string firstname;
    public string lastname;
    public string address1;
    public string address2;
    public string city;
    public string state;
    public string zipcode;
    public string custref;
    public string orderref;
    public DateTime appointment;
}
public class AppointmentInfo{
    public bool Accepted;
    public DateTime AppointmentDateTime;
    public string CompanyName;
}
}
```

As you can see in the preceding code, the three methods have no implementation, apart from returning the necessary data types. Now you can compile
the code and then retrieve the WSDL file in a browser by entering the URL to
the Web service with *?WSDL* appended to the end. The WSDL file for the Satellite Installation Web site looks like this:

```
<?xml version="1.0" encoding="utf-8"?>
<definitions xmlns:http="http://schemas.xmlsoap.org/wsdl/http/"
  xmlns:soap="http://schemas.xmlsoap.org/wsdl/soap/"
  xmlns:s="http://www.w3.org/2001/XMLSchema"
  xmlns:s0="http://fabrikam.com/XMLWSOrg"
  xmlns:soapenc="http://schemas.xmlsoap.org/soap/encoding/"
  xmlns:tm="http://microsoft.com/wsdl/mime/textMatching/"
  xmlns:mime="http://schemas.xmlsoap.org/wsdl/mime/"
  targetNamespace="http://fabrikam.com/XMLWSOrg"
  xmlns="http://schemas.xmlsoap.org/wsdl/">
<types>
  <s:schema elementFormDefault="qualified"
    targetNamespace="http://fabrikam.com/XMLWSOrg">
    <s:element name="GetAppointment">
      <s:complexType>
        <s:sequence>
          <s:element minOccurs="0" maxOccurs="1" name="cust"
            type="s0:customerinfo" />
          <s:element minOccurs="0" maxOccurs="1" name="ordertype"
```

```
          type="s:string" />
      </s:sequence>
    </s:complexType>
  </s:element>
  <s:complexType name="customerinfo">
    <s:sequence>
      <s:element minOccurs="0" maxOccurs="1" name="firstname"
        type="s:string" />
      <s:element minOccurs="0" maxOccurs="1" name="lastname"
        type="s:string" />
      <s:element minOccurs="0" maxOccurs="1" name="address1"
        type="s:string" />
      <s:element minOccurs="0" maxOccurs="1" name="address2"
        type="s:string" />
      <s:element minOccurs="0" maxOccurs="1" name="city"
        type="s:string" />
      <s:element minOccurs="0" maxOccurs="1" name="state"
        type="s:string" />
      <s:element minOccurs="0" maxOccurs="1" name="zipcode"
        type="s:string" />
      <s:element minOccurs="0" maxOccurs="1" name="custref"
        type="s:string" />
      <s:element minOccurs="0" maxOccurs="1" name="orderref"
        type="s:string" />
      <s:element minOccurs="1" maxOccurs="1" name="appointment"
        type="s:dateTime" />
    </s:sequence>
  </s:complexType>
  <s:element name="GetAppointmentResponse">
    <s:complexType>
      <s:sequence>
        <s:element minOccurs="0" maxOccurs="1"
          name="GetAppointmentResult" type="s0:AppointmentInfo" />
      </s:sequence>
    </s:complexType>
  </s:element>
  <s:complexType name="AppointmentInfo">
    <s:sequence>
      <s:element minOccurs="1" maxOccurs="1" name="Accepted"
        type="s:boolean" />
      <s:element minOccurs="1" maxOccurs="1"
        name="AppointmentDateTime" type="s:dateTime" />
      <s:element minOccurs="0" maxOccurs="1" name="CompanyName"
        type="s:string" />
    </s:sequence>
  </s:complexType>
  <s:element name="ConfirmAppointment">
```

```
        <s:complexType>
          <s:sequence>
            <s:element minOccurs="0" maxOccurs="1" name="custref"
              type="s:string" />
            <s:element minOccurs="0" maxOccurs="1" name="orderref"
              type="s:string" />
          </s:sequence>
        </s:complexType>
      </s:element>
      <s:element name="ConfirmAppointmentResponse">
        <s:complexType>
          <s:sequence>
            <s:element minOccurs="1" maxOccurs="1"
              name="ConfirmAppointmentResult" type="s:boolean" />
          </s:sequence>
        </s:complexType>
      </s:element>
      <s:element name="CancelAppointment">
        <s:complexType>
          <s:sequence>
            <s:element minOccurs="0" maxOccurs="1" name="custref"
              type="s:string" />
            <s:element minOccurs="0" maxOccurs="1" name="orderref"
              type="s:string" />
          </s:sequence>
        </s:complexType>
      </s:element>
      <s:element name="CancelAppointmentResponse">
        <s:complexType>
          <s:sequence>
            <s:element minOccurs="1" maxOccurs="1"
              name="CancelAppointmentResult" type="s:boolean" />
          </s:sequence>
        </s:complexType>
      </s:element>

    </s:schema>
  </types>
  <message name="GetAppointmentSoapIn">
    <part name="parameters" element="s0:GetAppointment" />
  </message>
  <message name="GetAppointmentSoapOut">
    <part name="parameters" element="s0:GetAppointmentResponse" />
  </message>
  <message name="ConfirmAppointmentSoapIn">
    <part name="parameters" element="s0:ConfirmAppointment" />
  </message>
  <message name="ConfirmAppointmentSoapOut">
```

```
      <part name="parameters" element="s0:ConfirmAppointmentResponse" />
</message>
<message name="CancelAppointmentSoapIn">
   <part name="parameters" element="s0:CancelAppointment" />
</message>
<message name="CancelAppointmentSoapOut">
   <part name="parameters" element="s0:CancelAppointmentResponse" />
</message>


<portType name="InstallSoap">
   <operation name="GetAppointment">
     <input message="s0:GetAppointmentSoapIn" />
     <output message="s0:GetAppointmentSoapOut" />
   </operation>
   <operation name="ConfirmAppointment">
     <input message="s0:ConfirmAppointmentSoapIn" />
     <output message="s0:ConfirmAppointmentSoapOut" />
   </operation>
   <operation name="CancelAppointment">
     <input message="s0:CancelAppointmentSoapIn" />
     <output message="s0:CancelAppointmentSoapOut" />
   </operation>
</portType>

<binding name="InstallSoap" type="s0:InstallSoap">
   <soap:binding transport="http://schemas.xmlsoap.org/soap/http"
     style="document" />
   <operation name="GetAppointment">
     <soap:operation soapAction=
       "http://fabrikam.com/XMLWSOrg/GetAppointment" style="document" />
     <input>
       <soap:body use="literal" />
     </input>
     <output>
       <soap:body use="literal" />
     </output>
   </operation>
   <operation name="ConfirmAppointment">
     <soap:operation soapAction=
       "http://fabrikam.com/XMLWSOrg/ConfirmAppointment"
       style="document" />
     <input>
       <soap:body use="literal" />
     </input>
     <output>
       <soap:body use="literal" />
     </output>
   </operation>
```

```
    <operation name="CancelAppointment">
      <soap:operation
        soapAction="http://fabrikam.com/XMLWSOrg/CancelAppointment"
        style="document" />
      <input>
        <soap:body use="literal" />
      </input>
      <output>
        <soap:body use="literal" />
      </output>
    </operation>
  </binding>

  <service name="Install">
    <port name="InstallSoap" binding="s0:InstallSoap">
      <soap:address location=
    "http://localhost/XMLWSOrg/Chapter5/InstallCompany2/install.asmx" />
    </port>

  </service>
</definitions>
```

You could describe the methods you need the remote Web services to
support in other ways, such as using a simple Word document, but giving the
installation companies a WSDL file has some benefits:

- **It is easy to do.**   Write the methods, compile the code, and then
  query the service for the WSDL file.

- **The WSDL file includes everything necessary.**   The proxy generator uses this file to build the proxy classes on a client for a
  remote Web service. Therefore, all the necessary information needs
  to be present.

- **The WSDL file can be used to verify the Web service created.**   If
  you compare the WSDL file generated by the remote Web service
  with this WSDL file, you should find them almost identical. The service port section, at the bottom of this WSDL file, will be different
  because it binds the methods to an actual URL.

Each remote installation company should use this WSDL file to implement
the Web service that you'll use from within your Web site.

If you have downloaded this book's sample files, you can look at the code
within the Web service of InstallCompany1 and InstallCompany2. Both solutions are located under Microsoft Press\XMLWSOrg\Chapter5. Each one implements the same WSDL file, but the actual code implemented in the methods is

different. Also, notice how the names of the services differ between the two solutions. For InstallCompany1, the service is named Install.asmx, and for InstallCompany2, the service is named Service1.asmx. Although you'll need to know this URL, changing the name of the service changes only the service port section of the WSDL file, which does not cause you any problems. The code contained in Install.asmx.cs for InstallCompany1 looks like this:

```
namespace InstallCompany1 {

    [WebService(Namespace="http://fabrikam.com/XMLWSOrg")]
    public class Install : System.Web.Services.WebService {
        public Install() {
            //CODEGEN: This call is required by
            //the ASP.NET Web Services Designer
            InitializeComponent();
        }

        //Component Designer generated code
        ⋮

        [WebMethod]
        public AppointmentInfo GetAppointment(customerinfo cust,
            string ordertype){
            if (cust.zipcode=="94101" | cust.zipcode=="94102"){
                Application.Lock();
                ArrayList activebookings;
                if (Application["ActiveBookings"]==null){
                    activebookings=new ArrayList();
                }
                else{
                    activebookings=
                        (ArrayList)Application["ActiveBookings"];
                }
                cust.appointment=new DateTime(2003,1,14,10,45,0,0);
                AppointmentInfo ai=new AppointmentInfo();
                ai.Accepted=true;
                ai.AppointmentDateTime=cust.appointment;
                ai.CompanyName="Install Company 1";
                activebookings.Add(cust);
                Application["ActiveBookings"]=activebookings;
                Application.UnLock();
                return ai;
            }
            else{
                AppointmentInfo ai=new AppointmentInfo();
                ai.Accepted=false;
```

```
            return ai;
        }

    }


    [WebMethod]
    public bool ConfirmAppointment(string custref,string orderref) {
        ArrayList activebookings=
            (ArrayList)Application["ActiveBookings"];
        for(int p=activebookings.Count-1;p==0;p--){
            customerinfo hc=(customerinfo)activebookings[p];
            if (custref==hc.custref && orderref==hc.orderref){
                activebookings.RemoveAt(p);
                Application.Lock();
                Application["ActiveBookings"]=activebookings;
                Application.UnLock();
                //
                // Any additional code necessary
                // when the appointment
                // becomes confirmed...
                //
            }
        }
        return true;
    }

    [WebMethod]
    public bool CancelAppointment(string custref,string orderref){
        ArrayList activebookings=
            (ArrayList)Application["ActiveBookings"];
        for(int p=activebookings.Count-1;p==0;p--){
            customerinfo hc=(customerinfo)activebookings[p];
            if (custref==hc.custref && orderref==hc.orderref){
                activebookings.RemoveAt(p);
                Application.Lock();
                Application["ActiveBookings"]=activebookings;
                Application.UnLock();
                //
                // Any additional code necessary
                // when the appointment
                // is rejected...
                //
            }
        }
        return true;
    }
}
```

```
public class customerinfo{
    public string firstname;
    public string lastname;
    public string address1;
    public string address2;
    public string city;
    public string state;
    public string zipcode;
    public string custref;
    public string orderref;
    public DateTime appointment;
}
public class AppointmentInfo{
    public bool Accepted;
    public DateTime AppointmentDateTime;
    public string CompanyName;
}
}
```

If you compare the specification of the earlier WSDL file to the methods defined in the preceding code, you'll see that they match. The preceding code does not make a complete solution, but it's enough for our purposes. This code will always return the same appointment data.

The code within the Service1.asmx.cs file for the InstallCompany2 Web service looks like this:

```
namespace InstallCompany2 {

    [WebService(Namespace="http://fabrikam.com/XMLWSOrg")]
    public class Install : System.Web.Services.WebService {

    public Install() {
        //CODEGEN: This call is required by the ASP.NET
        // Web Services Designer
        InitializeComponent();
    }

    //Component Designer generated code
    :

    [WebMethod]
    public AppointmentInfo GetAppointment(customerinfo cust,
        string ordertype){
        if (cust.zipcode=="98208" | cust.zipcode=="98207" |
            cust.zipcode=="98206"){
            Application.Lock();
            ArrayList activebookings;
```

```
            if (Application["ActiveBookings"]==null){
                activebookings=new ArrayList();
            }
            else{
                activebookings=
                    (ArrayList)Application["ActiveBookings"];
            }
            cust.appointment=new DateTime(2003,1,14,14,30,0,0);
            AppointmentInfo ai=new AppointmentInfo();
            ai.Accepted=true;
            ai.AppointmentDateTime=cust.appointment;
            ai.CompanyName="Install Company 2";
            activebookings.Add(cust);
            Application["ActiveBookings"]=activebookings;
            Application.UnLock();
            return ai;
        }
        else{
            AppointmentInfo ai=new AppointmentInfo();
            ai.Accepted=false;
            return ai;
        }


    }


    [WebMethod]
    public bool ConfirmAppointment(string custref,string orderref) {
        ArrayList activebookings=
            (ArrayList)Application["ActiveBookings"];
        for(int p=activebookings.Count-1;p==0;p--){
            customerinfo hc=(customerinfo)activebookings[p];
            if (custref==hc.custref && orderref==hc.orderref){
                activebookings.RemoveAt(p);
                Application.Lock();
                Application["ActiveBookings"]=activebookings;
                Application.UnLock();
                //
                // Any additional code necessary
                // when the appointment
                // becomes confirmed...
                //
            }
        }
        return true;
    }


    [WebMethod]
```

```
public bool CancelAppointment(string custref,string orderref){
    ArrayList activebookings=
        (ArrayList)Application["ActiveBookings"];
    for(int p=activebookings.Count-1;p==0;p--){
        customerinfo hc=(customerinfo)activebookings[p];
        if (custref==hc.custref && orderref==hc.orderref){
            activebookings.RemoveAt(p);
            Application.Lock();
            Application["ActiveBookings"]=activebookings;
            Application.UnLock();
            //
            // Any additional code necessary
            // when the appointment
            // is rejected...
            //
        }
    }
    return true;
}
}
public class customerinfo{
    public string firstname;
    public string lastname;
    public string address1;
    public string address2;
    public string city;
    public string state;
    public string zipcode;
    public string custref;
    public string orderref;
    public DateTime appointment;
}
public class AppointmentInfo{
    public bool Accepted;
    public DateTime AppointmentDateTime;
    public string CompanyName;
}
}
```

This code, from the Service1.asmx.cs file, looks similar to the code from the Install.asmx.cs file. The defined methods in these two files must be the same, and although a lot of the code within the methods is the same, there are differences. After all, this installation company covers a different set of postal codes. As long as the methods defined match those defined in the WSDL file, the implementations can vary. In our sample applications, these Web services are .NET based. Actually, as long as the methods defined are correct, it doesn't matter which Web service toolkit you're using to create the Web services or which platform the Web services are based on.

Examining User Interaction with the Satellite Site

Before we look at the code within the Satellite Site Web pages, we'll examine the user experience. When customers are ready to order a satellite system, they're directed to OrderPage.aspx. This page allows the user to enter personal information, such as his or her name and address, and to specify which satellite system to install. (See Figure 5-1.) This page should be secured using HTTPS because personal information is being passed over the Internet.

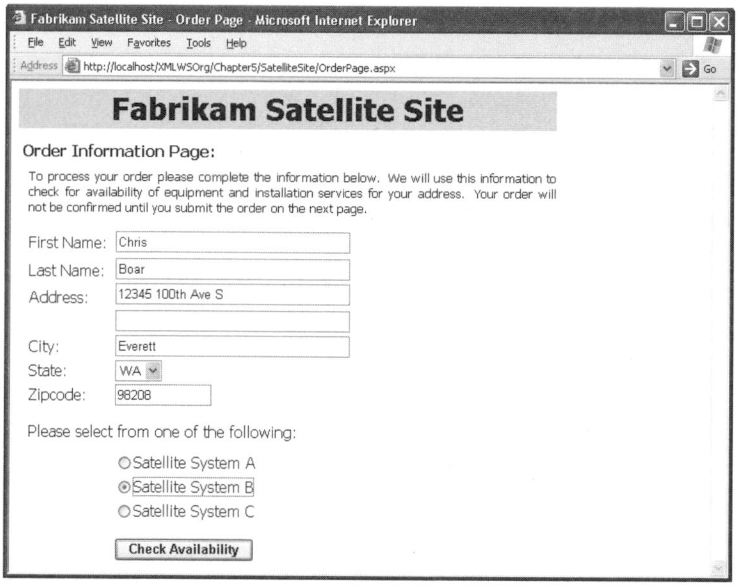

Figure 5-1   An example of a user completing the OrderPage.aspx page

Now the user clicks the Check Availability button. The Web site uses this information and queries the installation companies to see if they cover the area specified by the customer's address, which is done by matching the postal code. If an installation company doesn't cover the customer's address, the customer is presented with the RejectOrder.aspx page. If it covers the customer's address, the customer is presented with the ConfirmOrder.aspx page. (See Figure 5-2.) On this page, the customer can see the appointment date and time and the name of the company that will install the equipment. The customer can then confirm the order. If the order is confirmed, the customer is presented with the OrderComplete.aspx page. (See Figure 5-3.)

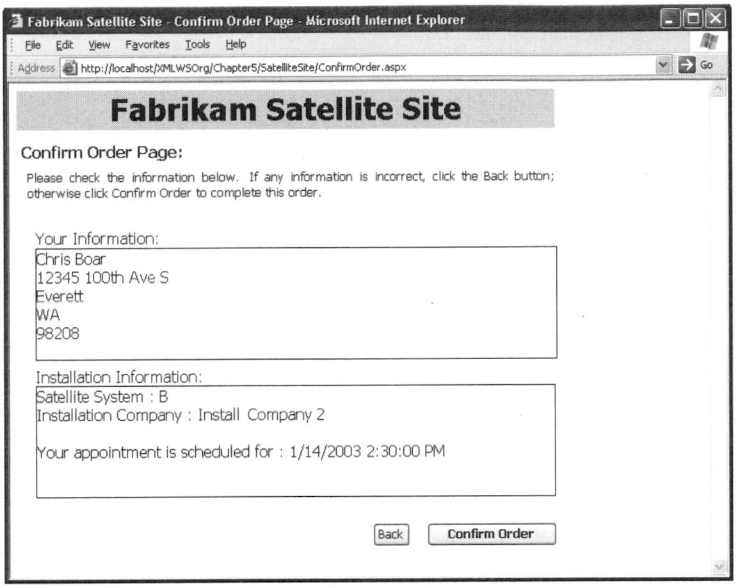

Figure 5-2   The ConfirmOrder.aspx page

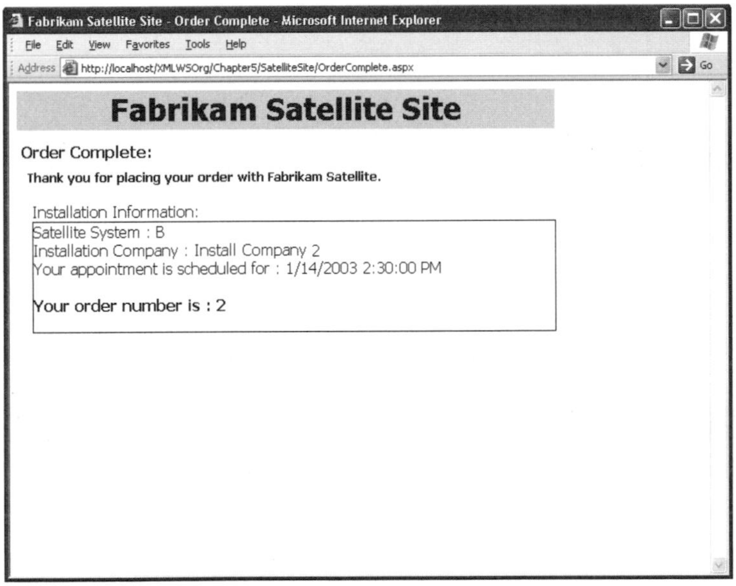

Figure 5-3   The OrderComplete.aspx page

With an understanding of the user experience, you can now look at what's happening between the Web site and the Web services of the installation companies. Figure 5-4 is a representation of the interactions between the Web site and two installation companies. There are seven steps spread over three Web pages, as the following figure shows.

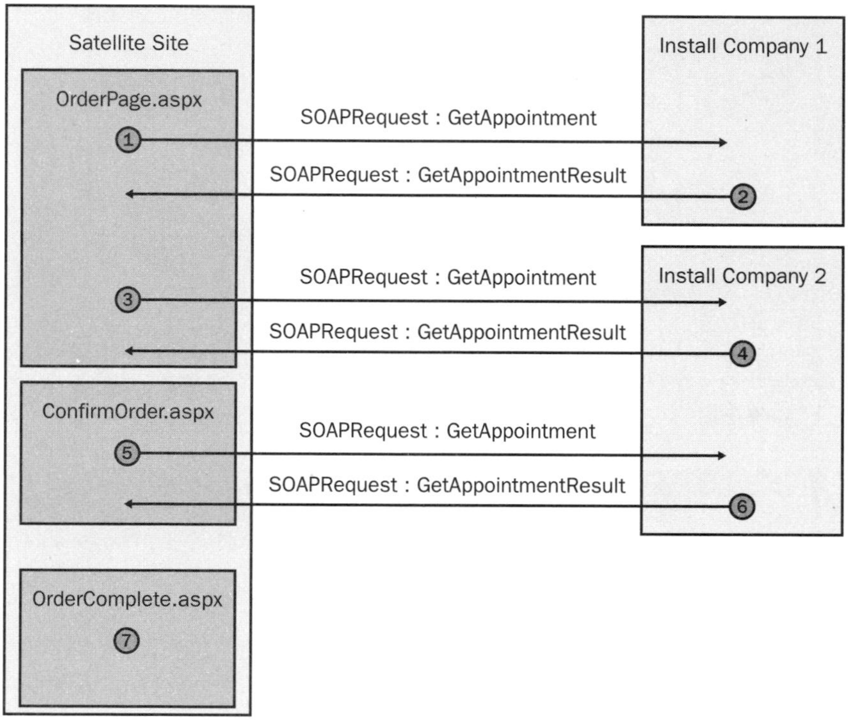

Figure 5-4 The Web site SOAP interactions

1. When the customer clicks the Check Availability button on the OrderPage.aspx page, the code associated with the click passes the customer information to the Web service of Install Company 1.

2. Install Company 1 receives the request and checks whether the postal code passed in the request is an area covered by the company. For the purposes of this diagram, we'll assume that the postal code is not covered by Install Company 1. The Web service sets the *Accepted* property of the *AppointmentInformation* object to *False* and returns the object to the Web site.

3. The OrderPage.aspx page receives this response from Install Company 1. Because the *Accepted* property is *False*, the code makes the same call to a different company using a different URL. This dynamic binding is something we have not covered in this chapter yet. We'll look at the code in the next section.

4. Install Company 2 receives the same customer information and checks the postal code. In this case, we'll assume that the postal code is covered by Install Company 2. The Web service gets the next available appointment date and time and builds an *Appointment-Information* object with the *Accepted* property set to *True* to return to the Web site.

5. The Web site receives the *AppointmentInformation* object and checks the *Accepted* property. Because *Accepted* is *True*, the customer is directed to the ConfirmOrder.aspx page. On this page, the appointment information is displayed and the customer can confirm the order. If the customer confirms the order, a call is made to the *ConfirmAppointment* Web method of the installation company that was able to accept the order.

6. Install Company 2 receives the order confirmation and changes the appointment in its own internal records to confirmed. Although not shown in this diagram, the installation companies also support a method named *CancelAppointment*. If the customer does not confirm the order, *CancelAppointment* is called to free up the appointment that was provisionally booked.

7. The OrderComplete.aspx page is displayed.

Setting a Web Service URL at Run Time

The OrderPage.aspx page is coded to call the same Web method of the two different remote Web services. As mentioned, the Web services for Install Company 1 and Install Company 2 both support the same Web method interfaces. Armed with this fact, the code can easily call the Web method of either company and get an expected response. To call the Web method of different Web services, you need to change the URL of the Web services at run time. You can accomplish this task by changing the *Url* property of the proxy instance you create. Look at the code for the *Click* event of the Check Availability button (*Button1_Click*).

```csharp
private void Button1_Click(object sender, System.EventArgs e) {
    if (Page.IsValid){
        Session["FirstName"]=txtFirstName.Text;
        Session["LastName"]=txtLastName.Text;
        Session["Address1"]=txtAddress1.Text;
        Session["Address2"]=txtAddress2.Text;
        Session["City"]=txtCity.Text;
        Session["State"]=lstState.SelectedItem.Text;
        Session["ZipCode"]=txtZipCode.Text;
        if (RadioButton1.Checked){
            Session["OrderType"]="A";
        }
        else if (RadioButton2.Checked){
            Session["OrderType"]="B";
        }
        else{
            Session["OrderType"]="C";
        }
        localhost.customerinfo CustInfo=new localhost.customerinfo();
        CustInfo.firstname=txtFirstName.Text;
        CustInfo.lastname=txtLastName.Text;
        CustInfo.address1 =txtAddress1.Text;
        CustInfo.address2=txtAddress2.Text;
        CustInfo.city=txtCity.Text;
        CustInfo.state=lstState.SelectedItem.Text;
        CustInfo.zipcode=txtZipCode.Text;
        CustInfo.custref="Fabrikam";
        Application.Lock();
        int ord;
        if (Application["OrderRef"]==null){
            Application["OrderRef"]=1;
            ord=1;
        }
        else{
            ord=(int)Application["OrderRef"];
            ord++;
            Application["OrderRef"]=ord;
        }
        CustInfo.orderref=ord.ToString();
        Session["OrderRef"]=ord;
        Application.UnLock();
        localhost.Install installWS=new localhost.Install();
        String[] WebServiceURLs=new String[2];
        WebServiceURLs[0]=
            "http://localhost/XMLWSOrg/Chapter5/"+
```

```
        "InstallCompany2/Service1.asmx";
WebServiceURLs[1]=
    "http://localhost/XMLWSOrg/Chapter5/"+
    "InstallCompany1/Install.asmx";
bool ok=false;
for(int p=0;p<2;p++){
    installWS.Url=WebServiceURLs[p];
    localhost.AppointmentInfo ai=installWS.GetAppointment
        (CustInfo,(string)Session["OrderType"]);
    if (ai.Accepted){
        Session["Appointment"]=ai.AppointmentDateTime;
        Session["InstallCompany"]=ai.CompanyName;
        Session["InstallURL"]=WebServiceURLs[p];
        ok=true;
        break;
    }
}
if (ok){
    Page.Response.Redirect("ConfirmOrder.aspx");
}
else{
    Page.Response.Redirect("RejectOrder.aspx");
}
    }
}
```

The URL of each Web service is held in an array, making it easy to step through each URL. The line of code that sets the URL of the Web service is shown in boldface. Setting the URL in code is a very powerful and yet extremely simple capability. The preceding code can easily be changed to support many more remote Web services by increasing the size of the array that stores the URLs and changing the *for* loop.

Note   Always keep in mind that these remote Web services could be implemented on any platform or hardware that supports our transport, which was HTTP and SOAP in this case. I mention this because the example code supporting this book all runs locally on your machine. You can easily forget that these services are normally remote, so their platform is effectively irrelevant.

Now that we've looked at indirect customer relationships, it's time to see how Web services can assist in direct customer relationships. You'll use the same basic set of Web service tools but with different clients.

Supporting Direct Business-to-Customer Relationships

How you connect directly to your customers depends on the nature of your product or service. The Microsoft software product Streets and Trips connects to a Web service to retrieve updated road construction information. A financial institution might want to allow its customers to check the value of their investments from their mobile phones. Your product might be a Global Positioning System (GPS) device that allows its users to periodically update the navigational data based on the data held on your servers.

Providing data to your customers can be as simple as creating the right Web pages on your site. But more and more these days customers are equipping themselves with mobile devices such as Personal Digital Assistants (PDAs), mobile phones, Pocket PCs, or other purpose-specific devices. Many of these devices can display Web pages, but for your customers to use your data, the device needs a connection to the Internet or to cache the page offline. You can provide your customer with a dedicated piece of software that caches your data on the local device, refreshing the data when a connection is available. This feature allows the user to benefit from your functionality even when a connection is not available. Web services are an ideal way to link from the remote device to your servers. The Microsoft Windows .NET Compact Framework allows you to use the power of .NET from either the Windows CE or the Pocket PC platform. Therefore, the great Web service functionality built into the .NET platform is available on these platforms. You might remember that allowing people to use their data anytime, anywhere, on any device is one of the original goals of .NET.

When developing a client application to be used by your customers, carefully consider which platform is most suitable. For example, an application that a user could use while shopping to track the cholesterol of items being purchased would not be helpful if it ran only on a laptop computer. It isn't easy to carry the laptop and groceries at the same time! A smart device application would be far more suitable. Also, if your application provides data that the user will want to carry out complex calculations on, a smart device would not be suitable because it is resource-limited.

Using the .NET Compact Framework

The .NET Compact Framework is a subset of the .NET Framework written to provide developers with a hardware-independent environment targeting resource-constrained devices. Visual Studio .NET 2003 integrates the .NET Compact Framework. Within Visual Studio .NET 2003, you can write applications in any installed language that target either the Pocket PC platform or Windows CE.

You can find considerable documentation on the similarities and differences between the .NET Framework and the .NET Compact Framework in Visual Studio .NET 2003. One thing to remember is that the .NET Compact Framework is targeted toward providing a rich client experience. Technologies such as ASP.NET are not part of the .NET Compact Framework. As you'll see in a moment, developing a .NET Compact Framework application in Visual Studio .NET 2003 is very similar to developing a Windows application. As you work with the different classes and controls, you might notice that not all support as much functionality as their full .NET counterparts. To make development easier, classes within the .NET Compact Framework use the same names as the equivalent classes in the .NET Framework. For example, the *TreeView* control exists in both the .NET Framework and the .NET Compact Framework.

Visual Studio .NET 2003 includes device emulator support. The emulator allows you to develop and test your smart device applications even if you do not have access to the actual hardware. Follow these instructions to build an application targeted for the Pocket PC platform:

1. In Visual Studio .NET 2003, click File, point to New, and then click Project.

2. In the New Project window, under Project Types, click either Visual Basic Projects or Visual C# Projects. Under Templates, click Smart Device Application.

3. In the Name field, enter a suitable name and then click OK.

   The Smart Device Application Wizard appears. This wizard allows you to specify the target platform and the type of application you want to create.

4. Under What Platform Do You Want To Target?, click Pocket PC.

5. Under What Project Type Do You Want To Create?, click Windows Application and then click OK.

Now you're ready to design the user interface, add any necessary code, and then test the application. Notice the list of controls in the Toolbox is slightly less than what's available when developing Windows applications. Add a button to the form, and double-click the button to add some code to the *Click* event, perhaps to display a message using

```
MessageBox.Show("A simple message")
```

To test the application, follow these steps:

1.   On the Debug menu, click Start.

2.   In the Deploy SmartDeviceApplication window, make sure the emulator entry is selected (which is the default) and then click Deploy.

The emulator window will appear. The device will launch, and the .NET Compact Framework will be installed on the device. Be patient; unless the device needs to be restarted, subsequent tests take less time because the device is already loaded with the .NET Compact Framework. When the button appears on the device screen, click it. You should end up seeing something like the application shown in Figure 5-5.

Figure 5-5   A simple Pocket PC application developed with Visual Studio .NET 2003 and the .NET Compact Framework

In the previous chapters, we've seen a number of uses for Web services in either Windows applications or ASP.NET applications. For the remainder of this chapter, we'll see how easy it is to integrate Web services into a smart device application.

Implementing the Wine Guide Client

The Wine Guide application is a Pocket PC application that allows the user to view a rating of a particular wine based on votes entered by users of the system. The user is presented with a tree view where the first level is the French wine-growing regions. Within each region, the major wines are listed, and then within each wine, a number of specific vintages are listed. Figure 5-6 shows how the user interface is represented.

Figure 5-6   The user interface of the Wine Guide application

Open the Visual Studio solution for this application at Microsoft Press\XMLWSOrg\Chapter5\WineGuideClientPPC.sln. With the solution open in Visual Studio .NET 2003, you can follow these steps to demonstrate the Wine Guide functionality:

1. On the Debug menu, click Start.

2. In the Deploy WineGuideClientPPC window, click Pocket PC 2002 Emulator (Default) and then click Deploy.

3. If this is the first time the Wine Guide has been run, you'll first see the Wine Guide : Set Server window. In the Server Name field, enter the name of your local machine and then click OK.

4. The normal Wine Guide window appears. Scroll through the list, and click South West.

5. After the wines for the South West region are downloaded, expand the South West node.

6. Click Gaillac.

7. When the vintages for the Gaillac region have been downloaded, expand the Gaillac wine.

8. Now click the Gaillac Rouge 1994 Mas de Bicary. Notice the rating the wine receives and the number of votes.

9. Select one of the five choices for the wine ranging from Bad to Great, and then click Submit Your Vote. Notice that the rating and number of votes change.

This application references a Web service named WineWebService. This reference was added in the same way references to other Web services have been made in previous applications: using the Add Web Reference tool. You can examine the Web service by opening the solution at Microsoft Press\XMLWS-Org\Chapter5\WineWebService\WineWebService.sln. The WineWebService supports the following five methods:

■ **GetRegions.** This method returns an array of the French wine regions.

■ **GetWines.** This method accepts an integer value that represents one of the wine regions and returns an array of wines for that region.

■ **GetVintages.** This method accepts the name of a wine and returns the vintages stored in the system for that wine.

■ **GetVintageScore.** This method accepts the name of a vintage and returns a complex type that includes the number of votes received for this vintage and the average of the scores from each vote.

■ **SetVintageScore.** This method accepts the name of one of the vintages held in the system and an integer score between 1 and 5.

In the client applications covered so far in this book, each call to a Web service has been *synchronous*; that is, the code makes the call to the Web service and waits for the response before continuing. In the following section, we introduce calling Web services asynchronously.

Calling Web Services Asynchronously

There are a number of reasons to call a Web service asynchronously. In the Wine Guide smart device application, the tree view is built using the results of multiple calls to a Web service. First the regions are loaded into the tree view. Then, as the user clicks on a region, the wines for that region are requested and added into the tree. If the user clicks on a wine, the vintages are then requested and added into the tree. By only requesting a part of the tree at a time, the size of the data being requested at any one time is reduced. However, more calls are made overall. When you consider that the bandwidth from the device to the Web service might be limited, calling a Web service synchronously could suspend the user interface and give the appearance of a hung application. By calling the Web service asynchronously, you can allow the application to continue responding. In this application, an activity bar is displayed until the response is received, informing the user that the application is waiting for the response. If you play with the application, you'll see that very few vintages are included in the data source (an XML file held on the server). Because the data in the file is minimal, downloading all of it at once would not be a problem. This application has been implemented this way deliberately to highlight the use of asynchronous Web service calls.

The first call made asynchronously in this client is contained in the *Form1_Load* procedure, as shown here:

```
⋮
localhost.Service1 ws=new localhost.Service1();
ws.Url="http://" + servername +
    "/XMLWSOrg/Chapter5/WineWebService/service1.asmx";
AsyncCallback ac=new AsyncCallback(this.UpdateRegions);
ws.BeginGetRegions(ac,ws);
⋮
```

This code is just the part of the procedure that deals with initiating the call to the Web service method, *GetRegions*. The first statement creates an instance of the Web service class. The second statement sets the URL of the Web service. Normally, for examples in this book, this statement would not be necessary, but because this Web service client is running on a smart device (albeit a device emulator), the Web service needs to be referenced by the name of the machine that hosts it. The third statement creates an instance of the *AsyncCallback* delegate using a reference to the procedure that should be called when the Web service response is received, which is the *UpdateRegions* procedure in this case.

The fourth statement actually initiates the call to the Web service. When the Add Web Reference tool creates the proxy class for the Web service client, it creates three methods for each Web service method. Within this proxy class, the synchronous method is named *GetRegions*. The other two methods support the asynchronous use of the Web service method. The method name to start an asynchronous call is the name of the method prefixed with *Begin*. The method that actually gets the result of the call, used in the *UpdateRegions* method, is the name of the method prefixed with *End*. Therefore, in this case, the name of the method to start the call is *BeginGetRegions*. This method requires two parameters, the *AsyncCallback* instance and an object referred to as the *asyncState*, which we'll use to hold the instance of the Web service.

Now the call has been made to the Web service, and execution continues. When the response is received from the Web service, the *UpdateRegions* procedure will be called. This client application uses a *Timer* control to animate the activity bar until the response is received. The code within the *UpdateRegions* method looks like this:

```
private void UpdateRegions(IAsyncResult ar){
    localhost.Service1 ws=(localhost.Service1)ar.AsyncState;
    string[] regions=ws.EndGetRegions(ar);
    timer1.Enabled=false;
    progress.BackColor=Color.White;

    foreach(string reg in regions){
        TreeNode n=new TreeNode(reg);
        treeView1.Nodes.Add(n);
    }
}
```

The method accepts a single parameter of type *IAsyncResult*. The first line of code within the procedure sets up an instance of the Web service proxy class by casting the content of the *ar.AsyncState* property back to the proxy class. The second line of code uses the *EndGetRegions* method of the Web service proxy instance to get the result of the Web service call. The rest of the method adds the results into the tree view control.

The client application asynchronously calls the *GetWines* and *GetVintages* methods. Calling a Web service synchronously or asynchronously is purely a client issue; no changes are necessary to the Web service itself.

Extra Credit

First cast your mind back to the indirect connections you looked at in the first half of this chapter. The code in the Web site OrderPage.aspx file stopped calling the installation companies once it received an accepted appointment. Can you think of a reason why you might want to call all the remote installation Web services and then pick one of the accepted appointments? On a broader level, will this ability to call a number of identical Web services map to a specific need within your organization? (For example, does your company utilize a product or service, such as road haulage or temporary staff, from more than one supplier?)

Now for an opportunity for extra credit based on the Wine Guide application covered in the second half of the chapter. As it currently stands, the application does not cache the data downloaded from the WineWebService to the local device. Your task is to add this offline functionality to the code and then test that it works. To simulate offline use, stop the Internet Information Services (IIS) service on your machine.

One last task I would like you to do is consider the level of smart device adoption in your organization. If the use of smart devices is low or nonexistent, consider if PCs are always the best solution for your business users. If you have users who need portable functionality, consider if a smart device such as a Pocket PC could be suitable. If it is, what are the obstacles to implementing on this platform?

Summary

All the examples covered so far in this book support the common Web service design where many clients use a single Web service. The Web site example used earlier in this chapter is different in that it demonstrates the use of Web services with a single client and multiple Web services. Although this use is perhaps less common, it's still a valid design.

The early part of this chapter discussed using a WSDL file to help your trading partners correctly implement a Web service that you specified. Once these remote Web services are implemented, you can use the *Url* property of the proxy class to dynamically reference a particular remote Web service.

Using the .NET Compact Framework, you can use your knowledge of .NET to write compelling smart device applications as easily as you develop Windows or ASP.NET applications. Whether you're programming for Windows or a smart device, you can use Web services to bridge the gap between the client and remote functionality.

Within the Wine Guide application, you saw how to call a Web service method asynchronously, which is not only powerful, but also fairly simple to implement. With asynchronous calls, you can continue to have a responsive interface while possibly time-consuming tasks are accomplished in the background. You're now prepared enough to turn to the next chapter and dig into securing your Web services.

6

Securing Web Services

In each code example we've covered so far in this book, we've focused on a particular business problem or feature of XML-based Web services. We've deliberately avoided including any aspect of security. Of course, when designing a Web service, a critical step of the process is deciding what security, if any, should be implemented. For each Web service, you should consider the following issues:

- **Authentication.** You need to decide whether it's important for you to know who it is that made the call to the Web service. For example, if your Web service provides public information about your company's products and services, you probably don't need to know who is requesting the data. In contrast, if you're accepting orders through a Web service, you'll need to know who placed the orders.

- **Authorization.** You need to decide whether different users of your service should have access to different functions of the service. For example, for a Web service designed for use within a corporate intranet, any authenticated user can submit expense reports using the Web service, but only managers can approve these expense reports.

- **Privacy.** You need to decide whether the data being passed from the client to your Web service should be protected from others being able to read this information. Privacy is definitely an issue on the Internet, but it can also be an issue over intranets. Remember, SOAP messages are made up of plain text, which is easily read by anyone with a little knowledge and inclination.

■ **Integrity.** You need to decide whether you should protect a message from being tampered with between the client and the server. It might not always be necessary to encrypt a message, but you might want a way to check whether the message has been corrupted since being sent by the client.

Before adding any of these functionalities to a Web service, you need to understand some basic cryptographic tasks.

Understanding Symmetric Key Encryption

With symmetric key encryption, data is transformed using an algorithm and a key (usually a long string). This type of encryption is *symmetric* because you can decrypt the data using the same key that was used to encrypt it. Therefore, to pass data between two parties with symmetric key encryption, each party must know the key. This key must be kept secure by both parties. If any third party discovers the key, that party can decrypt the data.

Symmetric encryption algorithms are also known as *block ciphers* because they process a block of data at a time. The symmetric algorithms provided in the Microsoft Windows .NET Framework use cipher block chaining, which means that the encryption of a block of data is affected by the previous block. To start the algorithm off, an initial data element, an Initialization Vector (IV), is required.

Understanding Asymmetric Key Encryption

Asymmetric encryption algorithms work with two keys that are related to each other. One key is kept secure, and the other key can be made freely available to others. The key that is not shared is referred to as the *private key*, and the shared key is referred to as the *public key*. Data encrypted with the public key can be decrypted only with the private key, which is very useful in establishing secure communication between two parties.

In Figure 6-1, Company A wants to pass the data *1234* to Company B without this data being visible to anyone while it's transferred over the network. In step 1, Company B gives Company A its public key. In step 2, Company A encrypts the data using Company B's public key. Finally, in step 3, Company B is able to decrypt the encrypted data with its private key.

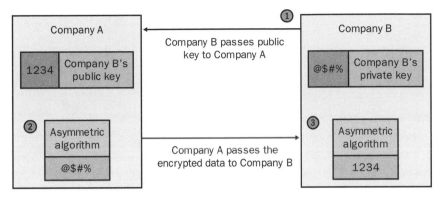

Figure 6-1   An example of secure data exchange with asymmetric encryption

What if a third party intercepts the public key while it's transferred over the network from Company B to Company A? Nothing happens because the encrypted data can't be decrypted with the public key. Only Company B can decrypt the data because only Company B has its own private key. If Company B wants to send data to Company A, Company B needs to get a copy of Company A's public key, encrypt the data, and send it to Company A.

Asymmetric encryption would appear to be more powerful than symmetric encryption, but asymmetric encryption has some limitations. First, asymmetric encryption uses a fixed buffer size, so it's not possible to encrypt streams of data. Second, asymmetric algorithms are more complex to compute than symmetric algorithms. The solution to the limitations of symmetric and asymmetric algorithms can be solved by using both asymmetric and symmetric algorithms in a cryptographic system.

Figure 6-2 details an exchange of information using both symmetric and asymmetric encryption. The goal is the secure exchange of data from Company A to Company B. As with Figure 6-1, in step 1, Company B passes its public key to Company A. In step 2, Company A uses the public key from Company B to encrypt a symmetric key. This symmetric key is generated for the sole purpose of encrypting the data that will be passed from Company A to Company B. When the connection is closed, the symmetric key will be discarded. In step 3, Company B uses its private key and the asymmetric algorithm to decrypt the symmetric key. Company A can now encrypt the data stream with the symmetric key, which is faster and better suited to a stream of data. Company B can receive this data and decrypt it with the symmetric key it received from Company A.

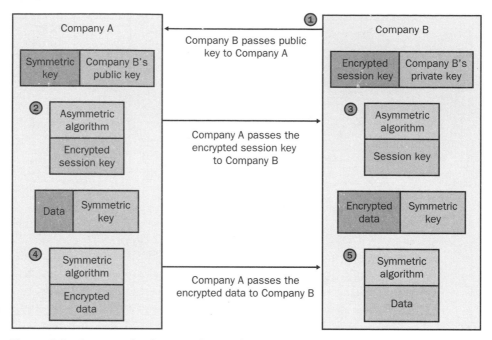

Figure 6-2   An example of secure data exchange using both asymmetric and symmetric encryption

Now that you understand the basic concepts of asymmetric and symmetric algorithms, it's time to look at how the .NET Framework provides cryptographic support. The *System.Security.Cryptography* namespace contains support for encrypting and decrypting data, generating hashes (which will be discussed later in this chapter), generating random numbers, and other cryptographic functions. To encrypt data for any Web service you create, you'll want to use classes from this namespace.

Using the Symmetric .NET Framework Classes

All implementations of a symmetric algorithm must inherit from the class *SymmetricAlgorithm*. You can use the following symmetric algorithms:

■ **The Data Encryption Standard (DES) algorithm.**   This algorithm is implemented as the abstract *System.Security.Cryptography.DES* class. You can use the DES algorithm through the *DESCryptoService-Provider* class.

■   **The RC2 algorithm developed by Ronald Rivest for RSA Data Security.**   This algorithm is implemented as the abstract *System.Security.Cryptography.RC2* class. You can use the RC2 algorithm through the *RC2CryptoServiceProvider* class.

■   **The Rijndael algorithm developed by Joan Daemen and Vincent Rijmen.**   This algorithm has been selected by the National Institute of Standards and Technology (NIST) as the Advanced Encryption Standard (AES) algorithm. (For more information, see *http://csrc.nist.gov/CryptoToolkit/aes.*) This algorithm is implemented as the abstract *System.Security.Cryptography.Rijndael* class. You can use the Rijndael algorithm through the *RijndaelManaged* class.

■   **The TripleDES algorithm.**   This algorithm uses three successive iterations of the DES algorithm, hence its name. You can use the *TripleDES* abstract class through the *TripleDESCryptoServiceProvider* class.

The symmetric algorithms are designed to process a stream of data one block at a time. Streams are implemented in the .NET Framework with the *Stream* class from the *System.IO* namespace. Common input and output choices, such as files and network connections, are implemented as classes that inherit from the *Stream* class. Therefore, it's straightforward to use the symmetric classes to encrypt data to a file using the *FileStream* class or to a network connection using the *NetworkStream* class. For encrypting the data that you'll want to pass with a Web service, you'll need a procedure that encrypts and decrypts a string. The following procedure uses the Rijndael algorithm to encrypt a string:

```
public static string SymmetricEncrypt(string str_to_encrypt,
    byte[] KEY,byte[] IV){
    byte[] bytes_to_encrypt=
        System.Text.UnicodeEncoding.Unicode.GetBytes(str_to_encrypt);
    RijndaelManaged r=new RijndaelManaged();
    MemoryStream ms=new MemoryStream();
    CryptoStream cs=new CryptoStream(ms,
        r.CreateEncryptor(KEY,IV),CryptoStreamMode.Write);
    cs.Write(bytes_to_encrypt,0,bytes_to_encrypt.Length);
    cs.FlushFinalBlock();
    long cslen=ms.Position;
    byte[] encrypted_temp=ms.GetBuffer();
    byte[] encrypted=new byte[cslen];
    for (int zz=0;zz<cslen;zz++){
        encrypted[zz]=encrypted_temp[zz];
    }
    return System.Convert.ToBase64String(encrypted);
}
```

The first thing to notice about this code is that it accepts a string to encrypt, as well as a key and an IV. Both the key and the IV are supplied as byte arrays. To encrypt the string using a symmetric algorithm, the string needs to be converted to a stream of bytes. The *Unicode* class within the *System.Text.Unicode-Encoding* namespace provides a method named *GetBytes* that converts a string into a byte array. The next line of code creates an instance of the *Rijndael-Managed* class. Because this procedure is not actually going to persist the encrypted data to any output device, an instance of the *MemoryStream* class is created. A *MemoryStream* class implements a stream using memory as its store. The data will be encrypted by writing the data to a *CryptoStream* object. This object will apply the cryptographic transformation, in this case an encryption algorithm, and then place this encrypted data into the *MemoryStream* object. The following line of code, copied from the previous procedure, creates the *CryptoStream* object:

```
CryptoStream cs=new CryptoStream(ms,
    r.CreateEncryptor(KEY,IV),CryptoStreamMode.Write);
```

The *CryptoStream* constructor accepts three parameters. The first is the stream on which the *CryptoStream* will operate, which in this case is the *MemoryStream* object. The second parameter is a transform object, which is any object that implements the *ICryptoTransform* interface. For this procedure, the transform object is supplied by using the *CreateEncryptor* method of the *RijndaelManaged* object. The *CreateEncryptor* method is passed the symmetric key and the IV. Finally the *CryptoStream* constructor needs to know what mode the stream will be used in. The mode can be either *CryptoStreamMode.Read* or *CryptoStreamMode.Write*.

Now that the *CryptoStream* object is created, the string data (now held as a byte array) can be written to the *CryptoStream* object using the *Write* method. It's important to call the *CryptoSteam* object's *FlushFinalBlock* method after writing the data into the stream. The *FlushFinalBlock* method is necessary because of the way the symmetric cipher works with blocks of data at a time. The encryption algorithm needs to be instructed that no further data will be entering the stream and that the last block should be encrypted into the stream. Because it's a block cipher, padding will be added to form a full final block.

Now the data is encrypted and held in the *MemoryStream* object. The remaining code in the procedure is used to generate a Base64-encoded string of the encrypted data. Base64 encoding is used to ensure that the string is suitable to be held in an XML document.

You might wonder why the array returned by the *MemoryStream* object's *GetBuffer* method is not simply passed into the *ToBase64String* method. The problem is that *GetBuffer* returns more than the results of the encrypted data.

To be able to successfully decrypt this data, it must remain at exactly the same length, that is, the same integer number of cipher blocks. In the process of turning the byte array into a string, if you add or subtract any data, you will not be able to decrypt the data. The code in the procedure uses the *Position* property of the *MemoryStream* object after the *FlushFinalBlock* method has been called on the *CryptoStream* object to trim the results of the *GetBuffer* method back to the correct length.

Decrypting encrypted data is essentially the same as encrypting. You use a *CryptoStream* object to apply a transformation to the encrypted data. The following procedure is the complimentary procedure to the *SymmetricEncrypt* procedure you just saw:

```
public static string SymmetricDecrypt(string str_to_decrypt,
    byte[] KEY,byte[] IV){
    byte[] bytes_to_decrypt=
        System.Convert.FromBase64String(str_to_decrypt);
    RijndaelManaged r=new RijndaelManaged();
    MemoryStream ms=new MemoryStream();
    ms.Write(bytes_to_decrypt,0,bytes_to_decrypt.Length);
    ms.Position=0;
    CryptoStream cs=new CryptoStream
        (ms,r.CreateDecryptor(KEY,IV),CryptoStreamMode.Read);
    byte[] decrypted=new byte[ms.Length];
    int bytesread=cs.Read(decrypted,0,(int)ms.Length);
    return System.Text.UnicodeEncoding.Unicode.
        GetString(decrypted,0,bytesread);
}
```

This procedure, named *SymmetricDecrypt*, accepts a string to decrypt, *str_to_decrypt*, and the necessary key and IV. The string must be encoded using the Base64 scheme. The *FromeBase64String* static method of the *System.Convert* class is used to get the data back into a byte array format. The symmetric algorithm instance of *RijndaelManaged* is created. You need to use the same algorithm to decrypt that was used to encrypt. As with the *SymmetricEncrypt* procedure, a *MemoryStream* object is created that will act as a temporary stream to hold the data being decrypted. However, in the *SymmetricEncrypt* procedure, data was written into the stream using the *CryptoStream* object's *Write* method. This time, because you want to decrypt the data, the data must be placed into the *MemoryStream* first and then read from the stream through the *CryptoStream*. In the following code, I've pulled out the important lines of code from the *SymmetricDecrypt* procedure:

```
    ⋮
    MemoryStream ms=new MemoryStream();
    ms.Write(bytes_to_decrypt,0,bytes_to_decrypt.Length);
```

```
ms.Position=0;
CryptoStream cs=new CryptoStream(ms,r.CreateDecryptor(KEY,IV),
CryptoStreamMode.Read);
byte[] decrypted=new byte[ms.Length];
int bytesread=cs.Read(decrypted,0,(int)ms.Length);
  :
```

After the *MemoryStream* object *ms* is created, the *MemoryStream* object's *Write* method is called to place the *bytes_to_decrypt* byte array into the stream. Then the *Position* property of the *MemoryStream* object is used to set the active position with the stream back to the beginning of the stream. After the *Write* method of the *MemoryStream* object has been called, the position will be at the end of the data written into the stream. Now the *CryptoStream* object *cs* is created using the default constructor. The first parameter is the *MemoryStream* against which the *CryptoStream* will operate. The second parameter is the transformation, which now is a decryption transform created from the *RijndaelManaged* instance using the key and the IV passed into this procedure. The final parameter informs the new *CryptoStream* that you'll be reading from the stream.

Now the code is ready to start actually decrypting the data. An array to hold the results is created, and then the *CryptoStream* object's *Read* method is called. The procedure uses the *GetString* method of the *Unicode* class to convert the byte array into a Unicode string to return from the procedure.

Generating Symmetric Keys

Both the *SymmetricEncrypt* and *SymmetricDecrypt* procedures require a key and an IV before they can encrypt and decrypt anything. Typically, algorithms support different key sizes, but the IV size is the same as the block size being used, which is sensible because the IV is used to initialize the block chaining. The following code exploits the *LegalKeySizes* property and the *LegalBlockSizes* property of the *SymmetricAlgorithm* class. The code will output to the console the legal key sizes and block sizes for the Rijndael algorithm. You can change the algorithm to any of the other symmetric algorithms provided by the .NET Framework and see the legal key and block sizes they support.

```
RijndaelManaged algorithm = new RijndaelManaged();
KeySizes[] legalkeysizes  = algorithm.LegalKeySizes;
KeySizes[] legalblocksizes = algorithm.LegalBlockSizes;
Console.WriteLine("Legal Key Sizes are:");
foreach(KeySizes v in legalkeysizes){
    int min=v.MinSize;
    int max=v.MaxSize;
    int skip=v.SkipSize;
    for(int ls=min;ls<=max;ls+=skip){
```

```
        Console.WriteLine(ls.ToString());
        if(skip==0)break;
    }
}
Console.WriteLine("Legal Block Sizes are:");
foreach(KeySizes v in legalblocksizes){
    int min=v.MinSize;
    int max=v.MaxSize;
    int skip=v.SkipSize;
    for(int ls=min;ls<=max;ls+=skip){
        Console.WriteLine(ls.ToString());
        if(skip==0)break;
    }
}
Console.ReadLine();
```

Running the preceding code produces the following output:

```
Legal Key Sizes are:
128
192
256
Legal Block Sizes are:
128
192
256
```

Any byte array of the correct length can be used for the key of a symmetric algorithm. When you create an instance of one of the symmetric algorithms, the key and IV properties of that instance are set to randomized key and IV values. You often create and use a key and an IV for only a single session, so using the values provided by the instance is often acceptable. You need to use byte arrays to hold a key or an IV, as shown in the following code:

```
RijndaelManaged algorithm = new RijndaelManaged();
byte[] key=algorithm.Key;
byte[] IV=algorithm.IV;
```

Another common task is generating a key for use in a symmetric algorithm from a password entered by a user. The .NET Framework provides a class named *PasswordDeriveBytes* to make this task easy, as shown in the following code:

```
byte[] salt = new byte[4] {50, 100, 125, 75};
PasswordDeriveBytes pwd = new PasswordDeriveBytes(txtPassword.Text,salt);
int bytesInKey = 16;
byte[] key = pwd.GetBytes(bytesInKey);
```

Before we move on to asymmetric encryption, the following code sample shows the *SymmetricEncrypt* and *SymmetricDecrypt* procedures being demonstrated in a simple console application. This demonstration code is available in this book's sample files at Microsoft Press\XMLWSOrg\Chapter6\Encryption\ConsoleDemonstration\SymmetricDemonstration\SymmetricDemonstration.sln. This simple example takes a string, encrypts it, and then decrypts it.

```
RijndaelManaged r=new RijndaelManaged();
byte[] key=r.Key;
byte[] IV=r.IV;

string str_to_encrypt="Mary had a little lamb...";
Console.WriteLine("Initial string: {0}",str_to_encrypt);
string encrypted_str=SymmetricEncrypt(str_to_encrypt,key,IV);
Console.WriteLine("Encrypted: {0}",encrypted_str);
string decrypted_str=SymmetricDecrypt(encrypted_str,key,IV);
Console.WriteLine("Decrypted: {0}",decrypted_str);
Console.ReadLine();
```

Using the Asymmetric .NET Framework Classes

Classes that implement asymmetric algorithms must inherit from the *AsymmetricAlgorithm* abstract class. The following two classes are provided that inherit from *AsymmetricAlgorithm*:

- The RSA algorithm, named after its inventors, Ronald Rivest, Adi Shamir, and Leonard Adelman in April 1977, has a class named *RSA*. This class is provided for developers who want to provide their own implementation of the RSA algorithm. To use the provided implementation, use the *RSACryptoServiceProvider* class.

- The Digital Signature Algorithm has a class named *DSA*. As with the *RSA* class, an actual implementation of this algorithm is provided through the *DSACryptoServiceProvider* class that inherits from the *DSA* class.

Although both the *RSA* and *DSA* classes provide asymmetric algorithms, the *DSA* class is specifically designed for digital signatures. We'll concentrate on the *RSA* class. The symmetric classes operate on streams of data. In contrast, the asymmetric classes accept a byte array to encrypt or decrypt. The length of this byte array depends on the size of the key being used. The formula is Maximum Array Size to Encrypt = (Keysize / 8) - 11.

For example, if the key size is 1024, the largest byte array you can encrypt is 117. The 11 bytes are necessary for padding. This size limitation is one of the reasons why asymmetric encryption is not used for large quantities of data. Another reason is that asymmetric algorithms are more processor-intensive than symmetric algorithms. The following code sample is a simple console demonstration of asymmetric encryption and decryption. You can find the solution for this demonstration at Microsoft Press\XMLWSOrg\Chapter6\Encryption\ConsoleDemonstration\AsymmetricDemonstration\AsymmetricDemonstration.sln. I'll cover the code in three blocks to make it a little easier to discuss. The first block of code drives the demonstration.

```
static void Main(string[] args)
{
    RSACryptoServiceProvider rsa=new RSACryptoServiceProvider();
    string PublicKeyInfo=rsa.ToXmlString(false);
    string PrivateKeyInfo=rsa.ToXmlString(true);
    Console.Write("Key size is: {0}",rsa.KeySize);
    Console.WriteLine(" therefore maximum input "
        +"array size is {0}",(rsa.KeySize/8)-11);

    byte[] a=new byte[10]{10,20,30,40,50,60,70,80,90,100};

    Console.WriteLine("Input array is: "+
        "10,20,30,40,50,60,70,80,90,100");
    Console.WriteLine();
    string encrypted=AsymmetricEncrypt(a,PublicKeyInfo);
    Console.WriteLine("Encrypted string is: {0}",encrypted);
    byte[] a_decrypted=AsymmetricDecrypt(encrypted,PrivateKeyInfo);
    Console.WriteLine();
    Console.Write("Output array is: ");
    foreach(byte v in a_decrypted){
        Console.Write(v.ToString()+",");
    }
    Console.ReadLine();
}
```

The first line of code within this procedure creates an instance of the *RSACryptoServiceProvider*. When the class is created, a public and private key are created automatically. Because the code needs to pass public and private keys to the encryption and decryption procedures later in the code, each key is placed into a string variable, *PublicKeyInfo* or *PrivateKeyInfo*, which is accomplished by the *ToXmlString* method of the *RSACryptoServiceProvider* class. The *ToXmlString* method creates an XML representation of the RSA key information. Its single parameter specifies whether the private key information should be included. The following code is an example of a public key represented as XML.

```
<RSAKeyValue>
  <Modulus>xjc1bgX3kaTyps7yZPo3ND2RAXch0WIYi2TX891jbU7BMp5dw8+M1k51v+
    EWQTnLEdrXPRZX002WeWYTD7wQk85RZGvWTQnGSA9YsksAx57onzoZ1Ab0CA7Jv5H
    FtNDryXttzoyegJtyn6bDcpDGjX0LwsuJLqBS/c6HaPFy5AE=</Modulus>
  <Exponent>AQAB</Exponent>
</RSAKeyValue>
```

Here's an example of a private key in XML:

```
<RSAKeyValue>
  <Modulus>xjc1bgX3kaTyps7yZPo3ND2RAXch0WIYi2TX891jbU7BMp5dw8+M1k51v+
    EWQTnLEdrXPRZX002WeWYTD7wQk85RZGvWTQnGSA9YsksAx57onzoZ1Ab0CA7Jv5H
    FtNDryXttzoyegJtyn6bDcpDGjX0LwsuJLqBS/c6HaPFy5AE=</Modulus>
  <Exponent>AQAB</Exponent>
  <P>9XQKmQKcQGCRwyHQOQgKMvxPXphQIenCW4Si4fAaeHAgSVqWnYsFhQ3VAQ+Go7D
    1VVu6VBvROoc8rZb4a6/CMw==</P>
  <Q>zruPB6bhM1CHn5U2cVPE81oViMPPq6NQiI+URRoX1a6nzh2erWamclWsom4RbUG
    uOjusI7kfqIe6yxrb6r6U+w==</Q>
  <DP>OEintXZ3xfte8VPrn2hMjmx09sgOd/hWbQ35G74nE78CaE+xgebDGUOWuGuLAD
    YsIGqsS2UlkTo5m8SmqmrfKQ==</DP>
  <DQ>jz/f6E12mvwePjJCu1x0iLvPWC126VQNJdN3xjpCccrIdEaKAVWz2F4NdbAXW0
    G73JYkvcw1Z65FfR9ra8oLqQ==</DQ>
  <InverseQ>ytgY3p+ad8dRFapPhdUGQYaZ4cRI2s0zFIkzLnYzIGB75q5PwHmJCblw
    h3mNUz17xBDCEGHXdl+bM7OrRRHunA==</InverseQ>
  <D>mZbiAdUB1os3suWckX4JFKO4HqiPPc2DM0/6ve4IQwTJU02/XiEO0NECqsHhGr2
    LitRGAAG2H/d456yejIyvUlojgR4aJOgolbgStgiOjDHxLNw8PtBT5Rko/QGnNiPgc
    nlgL1bicwqE5D6o+/wc5v8ps/jwKv7jHP2Zt8K+rdk=</D>
</RSAKeyValue>
```

As you can see from these two XML examples, the private key in XML contains the public key data as well as the necessary private key data.

The two lines shown in boldface are critical in the demonstration code sample. The first is the call to the *AsymmetricEncrypt* procedure. This call accepts the byte array to encrypt and the public key formation in XML. It returns the encrypted data as another byte array.

The second line in boldface is the call to the *AsymmetricDecrypt* procedure. As with the *AsymmetricEncrypt*, this call accepts the array to decrypt and the private key information. Its results are again a byte array.

All that remains now is to look at the two procedures, *AsymmetricEncrypt* and *AsymmetricDecrypt*. The *AsymmetricEncrypt* routine looks like this:

```
public static string AsymmetricEncrypt(
    byte[] to_Encrypt,string publickeystr){
    RSACryptoServiceProvider rsa=
        new RSACryptoServiceProvider();
    rsa.FromXmlString(publickeystr);
```

```
byte[] encrypted=rsa.Encrypt(to_Encrypt,false);
return System.Convert.ToBase64String(encrypted);
}
```

This procedure is very straightforward. An instance of the *RSACrypto-ServiceProvider* is created. The public key passed as a string into the procedure is loaded using the *FromXmlString* method. Finally the *Encrypt* method is called to encrypt the data. The resulting array is turned into a Base64-encoded string because we'll use this procedure in our Web services later.

The *AsymmetricDecrypt* routine, shown here, is very similar to the *AsymmetricEncrypt* routine:

```
public static byte[] AsymmetricDecrypt(
    string str_to_decrypt,string privateKey){
    RSACryptoServiceProvider rsa=
        new RSACryptoServiceProvider();
    rsa.FromXmlString(privateKey);
    byte[] bytes_to_decrypt=
        System.Convert.FromBase64String(str_to_decrypt);
    byte[] decoded=rsa.Decrypt(bytes_to_decrypt,false);
    return decoded;
}
```

The *AsymmetricDecrypt* routine differs from the *AsymmetricEncrypt* routine in that the input is a Base64-encoded string, so the byte array has to be recreated from the string. Another difference is that the routine uses the private key. Remember that it's not possible to decrypt the data using the public key that encrypted it; you must use the private key. A final difference is that the *Decrypt* method is called instead of the *Encrypt* method.

Generating Asymmetric Keys

The constructor for both asymmetric classes creates a new public and private key pair. You can specify the size of the keys in the constructor.

Asymmetric key sizes can vary depending on the algorithm being used. You can find out what the legal key sizes are using the *LegalKeySizes* method of the asymmetric algorithm you're using. The following code displays the range of legal key sizes allowed by the RSA algorithm as implemented:

```
RSACryptoServiceProvider algorithm = new RSACryptoServiceProvider();
KeySizes[] legalkeysizes   = algorithm.LegalKeySizes;
Console.WriteLine("Legal Key Sizes are {0} to {1} in steps of {2}",
    legalkeysizes[0].MinSize,legalkeysizes[0].MaxSize,
    legalkeysizes[0].SkipSize);
```

This code produces the following output:

```
Legal Key Sizes are 384 to 16384 in steps of 8
```

Now you have four procedures for encrypting and decrypting data using either symmetric or asymmetric keys. With these four procedures, you can start implementing a secure Web service. First you need to implement authentication and authorization within a Web service.

Implementing Authentication and Authorization

Authentication is confirming the identity of the entity attempting to use your Web service. In reality, you have no way of being absolutely sure who, or what, is making a request to your Web service. However, you can use a password and hope that the user of the password keeps it secure. Assuming that the user has kept the password secure, if a request is made to your Web service with a particular identifier and matching password that you have stored previously, you know it's the user you issued the password to.

Once you know who is accessing your Web service, you can logically determine what that user is or is not allowed to do with the service. If you're implementing a Web service for use within your intranet and you have a Microsoft Windows–based network, Windows authentication is an option.

Using Windows Authentication

Using Windows authentication is simple. However, you should be aware that you're using an authentication method that's tied to the transport (in this case HTTP) rather than using something within SOAP itself. If you need an authentication method that works within the SOAP message itself, perhaps because you want to send a SOAP message over a different transport such as SMTP, you can't use Windows authentication.

To enable Windows authentication, you need to disable anonymous access to the Web service file in Internet Information Services (IIS) by following these steps:

1.   Open Internet Information Services.

2.   Navigate through the folder structure to the Web service file (.asmx).

3.   Right-click the Web service file, and then click Properties.

4.   Click the File Security tab, and then click Edit under Anonymous Access And Authentication Control.

5.   Clear the Anonymous Access check box.

6.   Click OK twice.

The authentication mode specified in the Web.config file of the ASP.NET application needs to be set to Windows, which is the default setting.

You can access information about the user using the *User* property of the *WebService* class, as shown in the following code:

```
public string TestMethod(string domain)
{
    return "User.Identity.Name = "+
        User.Identity.Name+
        "\nUser.Identity.IsAuthenticated = "+
        User.Identity.IsAuthenticated.ToString()+
        "\nUser.Identity.AuthenticationType = "+
        User.Identity.AuthenticationType.ToString()+
        "\nContext.User.IsInRole("+domain+"\\WebService1) = "+
        Context.User.IsInRole(domain+@"\WebService1");
}
```

This simple Web method returns a string of information about the user. The important code is shown in boldface. You can access the name of the user account using *User.Identity.Name. User.Identity.IsAuthenticated* returns a Boolean value indicating whether the user is authenticated, which in this case must be *true. AuthenticationType* indicates what method of authentication was used to authenticate the user. The choices include Basic, NT LAN Manager (NTLM), Kerberos, and Passport.

For authorization, the *User.IsInRole* method can be very useful. With this method, you can determine whether the user is a member of a particular group defined in Windows. The preceding code determines whether the user is in the *WebService1* group. Your Web service might restrict access to only those users contained in a particular group. Therefore, you can control access to the Web service without having to reprogram it or implement a custom authorization module.

To access the Web service, the client will need to pass its credentials. The following code does just that:

```
localhost.Service1 ws=new localhost.Service1();
CredentialCache credcache=new CredentialCache();
NetworkCredential netcred=new NetworkCredential(txtUserName.Text,
    txtPassword.Text,txtDomain.Text);
credcache.Add(new Uri(ws.Url),"NTLM",netcred);
ws.Credentials=credcache;
MessageBox.Show(ws.TestMethod(txtDomain.Text));
```

An instance of the Web service proxy is defined as normal. Then the code creates a credential cache. This credential cache can store credentials for more than one resource and issue the correct credential for a resource when necessary. The credential cache needs to be loaded with the user and password information for the Web service. To do so, you create an instance of the *NetworkCredential* class, using the constructor to set the user name, password, and domain. Next you add the *NetworkCredential* instance to the credential cache using the *Add* method, specifying the Uniform Resource Identifier (URI) of the resource, the authentication type (in this case NTLM), and the network credential object. Now that you have a credential cache, you must remember the last step: linking the credential cache to the instance of the Web service proxy class, which is done by setting the Web service instance property *Credentials* to the credential class object.

You can test the preceding code yourself. Open the solution for the Web service at Microsoft Press\XMLWSOrg\Chapter6\Authentication\Windows\WebService\WebService.sln. The client code is located at Microsoft Press\XMLWSOrg\Chapter6\Authentication\Windows\WindowsClient\AuthenticationClient.sln. To run the client, follow these steps:

1. Disable anonymous access to the Web service file Service1.asmx using IIS.

2. Create a new local group on your machine named WebService1.

3. Add a new local user to your machine, and make the user a member of the WebService1 group.

4. Run the AuthenticationClient solution. In the Authentication Client window, enter the name of the user account created in step 3.

5. Enter the user account password.

6. Enter the name of your machine (the local domain name), and then click Test. You should see a message box that lists the user name, whether the user is authenticated, the type of authentication, and whether the user account is a member of the WebService1 group.

Windows authentication for a Web service can be a powerful tool, but it depends on the HTTP transport rather than part of the SOAP message itself. Although passing user credentials in the SOAP message itself is more work, it's ultimately more flexible because it has no dependencies on the transport.

Passing a User Identification and a Password in a SOAP Message

Placing a user identification and password into the SOAP message itself removes any dependencies on the transport. The Web service needs to check that the user identification is a known user identification and that the password matches the password stored for this user. Once the identity has been confirmed, additional logic can determine what access the Web service should allow. To make this system secure, the password sent in the SOAP message needs to be encrypted. One method of securing the password is for the Web service to provide a method that allows a client to retrieve an asymmetric public key with which to encrypt the password. The Web service can decrypt the password using its private key.

The following code is from a simple Web service that demonstrates receiving and decrypting a password passed to the service:

```
[WebService(Namespace="http://fabrikam.com/XMLWSOrg")]
public class Service1 : System.Web.Services.WebService {
    private static string PublicKeyInfo;
    private static string PrivateKeyInfo;
    public Service1() {
        //CODEGEN: This call is required by the ASP.NET
        //Web Services Designer
        InitializeComponent();
    }

//Component Designer generated code
⋮

    [WebMethod]
    public string GetPublicKey() {
        if (PrivateKeyInfo==null){
            CspParameters csparam=new CspParameters();
            csparam.Flags=CspProviderFlags.UseMachineKeyStore;

            RSACryptoServiceProvider rsa=new
                RSACryptoServiceProvider(csparam);
            PublicKeyInfo=rsa.ToXmlString(false);
            PrivateKeyInfo=rsa.ToXmlString(true);
        }
        return PublicKeyInfo;
    }

    [WebMethod]
    public string TestMethod(string userid,
        string encrypted_password) {
        string password=AsymmetricDecrypt(encrypted_password,
```

```
            PrivateKeyInfo));
        if (userid=="1001" && password=="Password"){
            return "Web Service Result";
        }
        else {
            SoapException se =new SoapException(
                "Authentication failed",
                SoapException.ClientFaultCode);
            throw se;
        }
    }


    public static string AsymmetricDecrypt(string str_to_decrypt,
        string privateKey){
        CspParameters csparam=new CspParameters();
        csparam.Flags=CspProviderFlags.UseMachineKeyStore;
        RSACryptoServiceProvider rsa=new
            RSACryptoServiceProvider(csparam);
        rsa.FromXmlString(privateKey);
        byte[] bytes_to_decrypt=System.Convert.
            FromBase64String(str_to_decrypt);
        byte[] decoded=rsa.Decrypt(bytes_to_decrypt,false);
        return System.Text.UnicodeEncoding.
            Unicode.GetString(decoded);
    }
}
```

As you read through this code, you'll see the implementation of the *Get-PublicKey* method. This method checks to see whether a public and private key pair have been generated and generates a new pair if they haven't. The code then simply returns the public key data to the caller as an XML string.

The method that's going to involve the authentication is called *Test-Method*. This simple method, for the purposes of this example, accepts only a user ID and a password as parameters. It's expected that the password has been asymmetrically encrypted with the server's public key. The first step is to decode the password with the server's private key. Next the user ID and password are validated. In this less-than-real-world example, this information is hard coded. In reality, it should be based on a list of users and passwords stored securely in a database or other suitable data store. If the user ID and password are authenticated, the Web service returns a simple string. Otherwise, a SOAP exception is thrown, indicating that the server was unable to authenticate the user based on the credentials supplied.

The remainder of the code defines the *AsymmetricDecrypt* procedure. This procedure is a little different from the *AsymmetricDecrypt* procedure discussed earlier in this chapter because it returns a string rather than a byte array.

This change was made to tailor the procedure to the needs of this particular example, in that the encrypted data is a password in the form of a string, instead of a symmetric key in the form of a byte array. The three lines of code shown in boldface instruct the cryptographic subsystem to use a machine-based crypto store rather than a user-specific crypto store. The context under which the ASP.NET Web service runs does not provide access to a user crypto store.

The example client application that uses the authenticating Web service is made up of two procedures: *button1_Click* and *AsymmetricEncrypt*.

```
private void button1_Click(object sender, System.EventArgs e) {
    //
    // First get the public key from the Web service.
    //

    localhost.Service1 ws=new localhost.Service1();
    string server_publickey=null;
    try{
        server_publickey=ws.GetPublicKey();
    }
    catch{
        MessageBox.Show("Unable to get the server's public key!");
    }
    if (server_publickey!=null){
        try{
            string encrypted_password=AsymmetricEncrypt
                (txtPassword.Text,server_publickey);
            MessageBox.Show(ws.TestMethod(
                txtUser.Text,encrypted_password));
        }
        catch (SoapException Error){
            MessageBox.Show("Error occured:" +Error.Message);
        }
    }
}
```

This code is called when the button on the client form is clicked. First, after creating an instance of the Web service proxy, the *GetPublicKey* method is called and the public key is stored for local use. The public key is then used to encrypt the user password. Finally the call is made to the *TestMethod* method of the Web service. The procedure that encrypts the password is similar to the asymmetric encryption procedures described earlier in this chapter, as shown in the following code:

```
public static string AsymmetricEncrypt(string str_to_Encrypt,
    string publickeystr){
    byte[] to_Encrypt=System.Text.UnicodeEncoding.Unicode.GetBytes(
```

```
        str_to_Encrypt);
    RSACryptoServiceProvider rsa=new RSACryptoServiceProvider();
    rsa.FromXmlString(publickeystr);
    byte[] encrypted=rsa.Encrypt(to_Encrypt,false);
    return System.Convert.ToBase64String(encrypted);
}
```

The code for this simple authentication example can be found at Microsoft Press\XMLWSOrg\Chapter6\Authentication\SOAP\ClientApplication\Client-Application.sln and Microsoft Press\XMLWSOrg\Chapter6\Authentication\SOAP\WebService\WebService.sln for the Web service. To confirm the security of the password being passed, it's worth looking at the actual SOAP messages exchanged between the client and the server when the button in the client application is clicked. Two request/response exchanges take place. First the client requests the server's public key. The request SOAP message looks like this:

```
<?xml version="1.0" encoding="utf-8"?>
<soap:Envelope xmlns:soap="http://schemas.xmlsoap.org/soap/envelope/"
  xmlns:xsi="http://www.w3.org/2001/XMLSchema-instance"
  xmlns:xsd="http://www.w3.org/2001/XMLSchema">
  <soap:Body>
    <GetPublicKey xmlns="http://fabrikam.com/XMLWSOrg" />
  </soap:Body>
</soap:Envelope>
```

The response SOAP message, supplying the public key information to the client, looks like this:

```
<?xml version="1.0" encoding="utf-8" ?>
<soap:Envelope xmlns:soap="http://schemas.xmlsoap.org/soap/envelope/"
  xmlns:xsi="http://www.w3.org/2001/XMLSchema-instance"
  xmlns:xsd="http://www.w3.org/2001/XMLSchema">
  <soap:Body>
    <GetPublicKeyResponse xmlns="http://fabrikam.com/XMLWSOrg">
      <GetPublicKeyResult>
        <RSAKeyValue><Modulus>4tbpxfjeLR+PLS/GpcQRBDJkmgfo+
          wSzNeBkDZ7YGUE8t6Ltrsa67bTDVotC5VYJw7mSXE3fmlsIKqK0j836jTo
          GvbYeLMmPVvpBC0S75qYiulkzy1+m+bHfGdxc+uKtwbt1BN2w8q/
          MkgT405PsCySyJqhm+WMATmt15KNPnnE=
          </Modulus><Exponent>AQAB</Exponent></RSAKeyValue>
      </GetPublicKeyResult>
    </GetPublicKeyResponse>
  </soap:Body>
</soap:Envelope>
```

Now that the client has the public key from the server, the password can be encrypted and the request can be made to the Web service method, as shown in the following SOAP request message:

```
<?xml version="1.0" encoding="utf-8"?>
<soap:Envelope xmlns:soap="http://schemas.xmlsoap.org/soap/envelope/"
  xmlns:xsi="http://www.w3.org/2001/XMLSchema-instance"
  xmlns:xsd="http://www.w3.org/2001/XMLSchema">
  <soap:Body>
    <TestMethod mlns="http://fabrikam.com/XMLWSOrg">
      <userid>1001</userid>
      <encrypted_password>sMXxrrlpp2AnV1yJSd9Y+g5/uhL5Rm6DuHvoB7BvKqjkyQ+
        dt/17Inq157gDCHvT+MMYZE293YlpbhVcqy1SC4qZmawSzqDYWWX9oWCbh
        GTgMidvdBhtmhiv1ILCiFz+aRMxtrF56Kguv8N40IZGt0xQT+w6XC6dzlwXrV9svTY=
      </encrypted_password>
    </TestMethod>
  </soap:Body>
</soap:Envelope>
```

Finally the response from the Web service from the server following the successful authentication of the user looks like this:

```
<?xml version="1.0" encoding="utf-8"?>
<soap:Envelope xmlns:soap="http://schemas.xmlsoap.org/soap/envelope/"
  xmlns:xsi="http://www.w3.org/2001/XMLSchema-instance"
  xmlns:xsd="http://www.w3.org/2001/XMLSchema">
  <soap:Body>
    <TestMethodResponse xmlns="http://fabrikam.com/XMLWSOrg">
      <TestMethodResult>Web Service Result</TestMethodResult>
    </TestMethodResponse>
  </soap:Body>
</soap:Envelope>
```

Before we leave the discussion of authentication for Web services, you might remember that I mentioned the use of SOAP headers for passing user and password information in Chapter 3. If you design a Web service where authentication is optional, using SOAP headers to pass authentication information is a great choice. It's also possible using ASP.NET to implement a custom *HttpModule* to trap the user and password information from a SOAP header and provide this information to the Web service method. Although this process is more involved, it's portable across multiple Web service methods. For more information on using an *HttpModule* for building a custom SOAP authentication mechanism, search in the Microsoft Visual Studio .NET 2003 help files for "Securing XML Web Services Created Using ASP.NET" and scroll down to the section titled "SOAP Headers – Custom solution." Also, in the preceding example, only the password is encrypted. A more secure solution would encrypt both the user ID and the password to prevent anyone looking at the message from discovering either the user ID or the password as the message is transferred over the network. If a hacker can read the user ID, all the hacker would have to do is crack the password.

Implementing Privacy

Effectively encrypting the password before sending it to the Web service ensures the privacy of the password. Anyone monitoring packets across the network should not be able to derive the password. So, using the methods described earlier, getting a public key from the Web service, using the public key to encrypt the data, and then sending it to the Web service can be enough to provide privacy for the data. This approach would not be efficient to encrypt a number of values. For example, consider the Satellite Installation Web site application discussed in Chapter 5. A request from the Satellite Installation Web site to one of the installation companies looks like this:

```xml
<?xml version="1.0" encoding="utf-8"?>
<soap:Envelope xmlns:soap="http://schemas.xmlsoap.org/soap/envelope/"
  xmlns:xsi="http://www.w3.org/2001/XMLSchema-instance"
  xmlns:xsd="http://www.w3.org/2001/XMLSchema">
  <soap:Body>
    <GetAppointment xmlns="http://fabrikam.com/XMLWSOrg">
      <cust>
        <firstname>Chris</firstname>
        <lastname>Boar</lastname>
        <address1>19019 1St Ave NE</address1>
        <address2 />
        <city>Bellevue</city>
        <state>WA</state>
        <zipcode>98208</zipcode>
        <custref>Fabrikam</custref>
        <orderref>1</orderref>
        <appointment>0001-01-01T00:00:00.0000000-08:00</appointment>
      </cust>
      <ordertype>B</ordertype>
    </GetAppointment>
  </soap:Body>
</soap:Envelope>
```

Within this SOAP request, it's the *Cust* element that needs encryption because it holds the sensitive customer information. The remainder of the SOAP message can be safely sent as is. Encrypting the *Cust* element would not be hard if you could get to the SOAP message after the framework creates it in the proxy but before it's sent over the network. The .NET Framework *SoapExtension* class makes it possible to process a SOAP message during different stages.

Introducing the *SoapExtension* Class

The *SoapExtension* class allows you to hook your own code into the processing that takes place to convert an object into a SOAP message and then send it across the network. It also allows you to do the same thing when a SOAP message is received.

You use the *SoapExtension* class by creating a class of your own that inherits the *SoapExtension* class. Your class should provide an implementation of each of the *SoapExtension* class's four methods: *GetInitializer*, *Initialize*, *ChainStream*, and *ProcessMessage*.

The *SoapExtension* class has three methods for initializing data, and each has a different purpose.

- **Constructor.**   Called each time an instance of the *SoapExtension* class is instantiated.

- **GetInitializer.**   Called only the first time a call is made to the Web service, which provides you with an opportunity to set some data that ASP.NET caches and then supplies to *SoapExtension* on each subsequent use of the class through the *Initialize* method.

- **Initialize.**   Similar to the class constructor in that it's called each time an instance is created. However, it receives whatever object was returned from the *GetInitializer* method.

The use of *GetInitializer* and *Initialize* have to do with performance. You can set up some data once in the *GetInitializer* method that's then supplied to all subsequent creations of the Web service method. You'll see this implemented in the example code in the section "Implementing Privacy in the Satellite Installation Application" later in this chapter.

The *ChainStream* method allows you access to the data stream itself. You should save a reference to the stream passed into the *ChainStream* method and also return a reference to a new *MemoryStream* object. It's important to understand that when a Web service receives a SOAP request, the stream reference passed into *ChainStream* contains the serialized SOAP request at the stage just before a SOAP message is deserialized from the SOAP message sent across the network into an object. The stream reference you return from *ChainStream* is used by the .NET Framework to write the serialized SOAP message at the stage just after a SOAP message is serialized but before the SOAP message is sent over the network. The *SoapExtension* class provides you with four opportunities to manipulate this process, as shown in Figure 6-3.

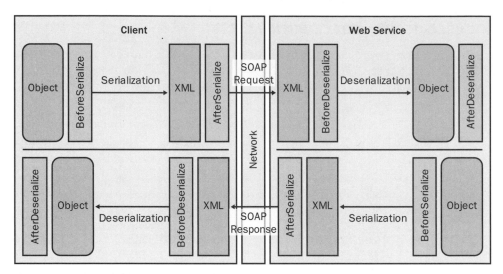

Figure 6-3 The SOAP processing flow and *SoapExtension* message stages

You can use the *ProcessMessage* method of the *SoapExtension* class to gain access to the stream of the SOAP message at the following four stages:

- **SoapMessageStage.BeforeSerialize.** Takes place before the object has been converted into a SOAP message.

- **SoapMessageStage.AfterSerialize.** Takes place after the object has been converted into a SOAP message but before the SOAP message is sent over the wire.

- **SoapMessageStage.BeforeDeserialize.** Takes place when a SOAP message is received from the network but before the SOAP message is deserialized into an object.

- **SoapMessageStage.AfterDeserialize.** Takes place after the received SOAP message has been deserialized into an object.

Introducing the *SoapExtensionAttribute* Class

You can have more than one class that inherits from the *SoapExtension* class. To inform the .NET Framework which of your Web methods should use which *SoapExtension*, you use attributes. The .NET Framework allows you to create your own custom attributes. To define an attribute as a link to a *SoapExtension* class, you create a class that inherits from the *SoapExtensionAttribute* class. The following code is an example of defining a custom *SoapExtensionAttribute* that will allow you to indicate that a Web method should encrypt or decrypt some data within the SOAP message:

```
[AttributeUsage(AttributeTargets.Method)]
public class CryptoExtensionAttribute : SoapExtensionAttribute{
    public CryptoParams cryptoparams;
    private int m_priority;
    public override System.Type ExtensionType {
        get {
            return typeof(CryptoExtension);
        }
    }

    public override int Priority {
        get {
            return m_priority;
        }
        set {
            m_priority=value;
        }
    }
    public CryptoExtensionAttribute(string encryptnode,
        string decryptnode,string wsnamespace){
        cryptoparams=new CryptoParams();
        cryptoparams.m_encryptnode=encryptnode;
        cryptoparams.m_decryptnode=decryptnode;
        cryptoparams.m_namespace=wsnamespace;
    }
}
```

Notice that the class itself is attributed with *AttributeUsage* to indicate that the class defines an attribute that must be used against a method. The class is called *CryptoExtensionAttribute*, and it inherits the *SoapExtensionAttribute* class. The class must implement the *ExtensionType* property and the *Priority* property. The *ExtensionType* property should return the type of the class that inherits from *SoapExtension*, which is a class named *CryptoExtension*. The *Priority* property should allow an internal variable (*m_priority*) to be set and retrieved. In the class constructor, the parameters are stored in a single object. These parameters will be needed later in the class that implements the *Soap-Extension* itself, and having the data in a single object makes it easier to use these parameters.

Now that the *CryptoExtensionAttribute* is defined, you can use it to mark a Web method as using the *CryptoExtension* class, as shown in the following code:

```
[WebMethod]
[CryptoExtension("AppointmentDateTime","cust",
    "http://fabrikam.com/XMLWSOrg")]
public AppointmentInfo GetAppointment(customerinfo cust,
    string ordertype){
⋮
```

This method has the *[WebMethod]* attribute defined against it, which informs the system that this method should be made available as a Web service method. The *CryptoExtension* attribute informs the system that this Web method uses the *SoapExtension* implementation as defined in *SoapExtensionAttribute*.

Now you have the major components needed to write the code that will encrypt and decrypt whole elements of a SOAP message. One of the advantages of using the *SoapExtension* class is that the functionality provided can be linked with little difficulty to other Web methods of your Web service.

Implementing Privacy in the Satellite Installation Application

The Satellite Installation Web site, first introduced in Chapter 5, consists of a Web site that allows customers to order a satellite system. Once the customer's name and address have been entered, the Web site uses a Web service of two satellite installation companies to determine whether the customer is within their service coverage area. If the customer can be serviced by either installation company, the Web service response includes the date and time of the installation appointment. At this point, the appointment is provisional and depends on the customer confirming the order. If the order is confirmed, the Satellite Installation Web site uses another Web service with the appropriate installation company to confirm the installation appointment. As this system was left in Chapter 5, the data in the SOAP messages, which includes personal information, are sent as plain text.

Let's examine implementing data privacy at the Web server for this system. If you have downloaded this book's sample files, you can open the InstallCompany1 Web service at Microsoft Press\XMLWSOrg\Chapter6\Encryption\InstallCompany1\InstallCompany1.sln. The following code is from the Install.asmx.cs file. I have used boldfaced type to mark the new lines of code added to the original solution from Chapter 5.

```
using System;
using System.Collections;
using System.ComponentModel;
```

```csharp
using System.Data;
using System.Diagnostics;
using System.Web;
using System.Web.Services;
using System.Web.Services.Protocols;
using System.Security.Cryptography;

namespace InstallCompany1 {
    /// <summary>
    /// Summary description for Service1.
    /// </summary>
    [WebService(Namespace="http://fabrikam.com/XMLWSOrg")]
    public class Install : System.Web.Services.WebService {
        public static string PrivateKeyInfo;
        public static string PublicKeyInfo;
        public RSAHeader rsaheader;

        public Install() {
            //CODEGEN: This call is required by the ASP.NET
            //Web Services Designer
            InitializeComponent();
        }

        // Component Designer generated code
        ⋮

        [WebMethod]
        [CryptoExtension("AppointmentDateTime","cust",
            "http://fabrikam.com/XMLWSOrg")]
        [SoapHeader("rsaheader",Required=false)]
        public AppointmentInfo GetAppointment(
            customerinfo cust,string ordertype){
            if (cust.zipcode=="94101" | cust.zipcode=="94102"){
                Application.Lock();
                ArrayList activebookings;
                if (Application["ActiveBookings"]==null){
                    activebookings=new ArrayList();
                }
                else{
                    activebookings=(ArrayList)
                        Application["ActiveBookings"];
                }
                cust.appointment=new DateTime(2003,1,14,10,45,0,0);
                AppointmentInfo ai=new AppointmentInfo();
                ai.Accepted=true;
                ai.AppointmentDateTime=cust.appointment;
                ai.CompanyName="Install Company 1";
                activebookings.Add(cust);
```

```
            Application["ActiveBookings"]=activebookings;
            Application.UnLock();
            return ai;
        }
        else{
            AppointmentInfo ai=new AppointmentInfo();
            ai.Accepted=false;
            return ai;
        }

    }


    [WebMethod]
    public bool ConfirmAppointment(string custref,string orderref) {
        ArrayList activebookings=(ArrayList)
            Application["ActiveBookings"];
        for(int p=activebookings.Count-1;p==0;p--){
            customerinfo hc=(customerinfo)activebookings[p];
            if (custref==hc.custref && orderref==hc.orderref){
                activebookings.RemoveAt(p);
                Application.Lock();
                Application["ActiveBookings"]=activebookings;
                Application.UnLock();
                //
                // Any additional code necessary when the appointment
                // becomes confirmed...
                //
            }
        }
        return true;
    }


    [WebMethod]
    public bool CancelAppointment
        (string custref,string orderref){
        ArrayList activebookings=(ArrayList)
            Application["ActiveBookings"];
        for(int p=activebookings.Count-1;p==0;p--){
            customerinfo hc=(customerinfo)activebookings[p];
            if (custref==hc.custref && orderref==hc.orderref){
                activebookings.RemoveAt(p);
                Application.Lock();
                Application["ActiveBookings"]=activebookings;
                Application.UnLock();
                //
                // Any additional code necessary
                // when the appointment
                // is rejected...
```

```
            //
        }
    }
    return true;
}
[WebMethod]
public string GetPublicKey(){
    if (Install.PrivateKeyInfo==null){
        CspParameters csparam=new CspParameters();
        csparam.Flags=CspProviderFlags.UseMachineKeyStore;

        RSACryptoServiceProvider rsa=
            new RSACryptoServiceProvider(csparam);
        Install.PublicKeyInfo=rsa.ToXmlString(false);
        Install.PrivateKeyInfo=rsa.ToXmlString(true);
    }

    return PublicKeyInfo;
}
}
public class customerinfo{
    public string firstname;
    public string lastname;
    public string address1;
    public string address2;
    public string city;
    public string state;
    public string zipcode;
    public string custref;
    public string orderref;
    public DateTime appointment;
}
public class AppointmentInfo{
    public bool Accepted;
    public DateTime AppointmentDateTime;
    public string CompanyName;
}
}
```

Apart from including some namespaces and declaring some variables, the two biggest additions to the code are the attributes to the *GetAppointment* method and the new Web method *GetPublicKey*. First two new attributes, *CryptoExtension* and *SoapHeader*, are added.

The *CrytoExtension* attribute of the *GetAppointment* method indicates to the *CryptoExtension* code that the element of the SOAP response *AppointmentDateTime* should be encrypted, that the inbound element of the SOAP request *cust* should be decrypted, and that the namespace for the message is *http://fabrikam.com/XMLWSOrg*, as shown in this code:

```
[CryptoExtension("AppointmentDateTime","cust",
    "http://fabrikam.com/XMLWSOrg")]
```

The *SoapHeader* attribute specifies that a *SoapHeader* as defined by the class referenced by *rsaheader* can be supplied with the SOAP request. This header, if present, will contain the encryption key. You'll see how this key information is extracted in the *CryptoExtension* class later.

The second addition to the code is the *GetPublicKey* method. This method is necessary to allow the client application to retrieve an asymmetric public key. Because the amount of data you can encrypt with an asymmetric algorithm is limited by the key length and the size of the data to be encrypted will vary, this implementation will use both asymmetric and symmetric encryption. The client will retrieve a public key from the server and use it to encrypt a symmetric key, often referred to as the *session key*. The data is then encrypted using the symmetric session key. Then the SOAP request, containing the encrypted data, is passed with a SOAP header that contains the asymmetrically encrypted session key. The server will then be able to decrypt the session key using its private asymmetric key and then decrypt the actual data in the SOAP message using the symmetric session key.

The actual changes to the Install.asmx.cs file are not large. Perhaps the most significant thing to notice is that the code within the *GetAppointment* method does *not* change. The encryption and decryption will be dealt with before the data reaches the method.

The majority of the code to enable this secure exchange of information is held in the ServerCrypto.cs file. Rather than reproduce all the code here, I'll introduce a section at a time. To see the entire file, open the solution at Microsoft Press\XMLWSOrg\Chapter6\Encryption\InstallCompany1\InstallCompany1.sln, and then open the ServerCrypto.cs file. Most of the code is contained in the *ProcessMessage* method of the *CryptoExtension* class, but before any processing can take place, *ChainStream* needs to be implemented to allow access to the data.

```
public override System.IO.Stream ChainStream(System.IO.Stream stream) {
    networkstream=stream;
    newstream=new MemoryStream();
    return newstream;
}
```

This code saves a reference to the stream passed into the *ChainStream* method and returns a new *MemoryStream* reference named *newstream*.

The code implemented in the *GetInitializer* methods and *Initialize* method looks like this:

```
public override object GetInitializer(
    System.Web.Services.Protocols.LogicalMethodInfo methodInfo,
    System.Web.Services.Protocols.SoapExtensionAttribute attribute) {
    return ((CryptoExtensionAttribute)attribute).cryptoparams;
}

public override object GetInitializer(System.Type serviceType) {
    return null;
}

public override void Initialize(object initializer) {
    cryptoparams=(CryptoParams)initializer;
}
```

The code in the first *GetInitializer* method simply returns the object contained in the *cryptoparams* property of the *CryptoExtensionAttribute*. This object is used to pass the data provided in the *CryptoExtension* attribute for the Web method through to the *CryptoExtension* instance. You'll see the code that sets up the *cryptoparams* object later in this section. The *Initialize* method simply returns the same object as set up by the *GetInitializer* method.

Now let's examine the *ProcessMessage* method of the *CryptoExtension* class, which inherits from the *SoapExtension* class.

```
public override void ProcessMessage
    (System.Web.Services.Protocols.SoapMessage message) {
    switch (message.Stage){
        case SoapMessageStage.BeforeDeserialize:
            //
            // Set up newstream.
            //
            Copy(networkstream,newstream);
            newstream.Position=0;
            //
            // Load the stream into a Document Object Model.
            //
            XmlTextReader xreader =new XmlTextReader(newstream);
            XmlDocument dom=new XmlDocument();
            dom.Load(xreader);
            XmlNamespaceManager nsmgr=
                new XmlNamespaceManager(dom.NameTable);
            nsmgr.AddNamespace("dn",cryptoparams.m_namespace);
            if (cryptoparams.m_encryptnode!="" |
                cryptoparams.m_decryptnode!=""){
                //
                // If data is encrypted, we need to get the
                // KEY and IV. These should be present in the
                // SOAP header.
                //
```

```
        //
        XmlNode RSANode=
            dom.SelectSingleNode(@"//dn:RSAHeader",nsmgr);
        if (RSANode!=null){
            symmetricKey=AsymmetricDecrypt(
                RSANode.SelectSingleNode(
                    @"//dn:EncryptedSymmetricKey",
                    nsmgr).InnerText,Install.PrivateKeyInfo);
            symmetricIV=AsymmetricDecrypt(
                RSANode.SelectSingleNode(
                    @"//dn:EncryptedSymmetricIV",
                    nsmgr).InnerText,Install.PrivateKeyInfo);
        }
    }
    //
    // Check to see if there is data that should be decrypted.
    //
    if (cryptoparams.m_decryptnode!=""){
        //
        // Retrieve the node contents to be decrypted.
        //
        XmlNode node=dom.SelectSingleNode(
            @"//dn:"+cryptoparams.m_decryptnode,nsmgr);
        //
        // Decrypt the data.
        //
        string dec_str=SymmetricDecrypt(
            node.InnerText,symmetricKey,symmetricIV);
        node.InnerXml=dec_str;
        //
        // Return the XML to a stream and copy
        // to the newstream.
        //
        MemoryStream decryptedstream=new MemoryStream();
        dom.Save(decryptedstream);
        decryptedstream.Position=0;
        newstream.SetLength(0);
        Copy(decryptedstream,newstream);
        newstream.Position=0;
    }
    newstream.Position=0;
    break;
case SoapMessageStage.AfterDeserialize:
    break;
case SoapMessageStage.BeforeSerialize:
    break;
case SoapMessageStage.AfterSerialize:
    //
```

```
// AfterSerialize is called after outbound
// data is turned into a SOAP message.
//
newstream.Position=0;
//
// First check if part of the SOAP
// message should be encrypted.
// Also check if we have a public key to encrypt with.
//
if (cryptoparams.m_encryptnode!=""){
    //
    // First get stream contents into a
    // Document Object Model.
    //
    XmlTextReader enc_xreader =
        new XmlTextReader(newstream);
    XmlDocument dom2=new XmlDocument();
    dom2.Load(enc_xreader);
    XmlNamespaceManager nsmgr2=
        new XmlNamespaceManager(dom2.NameTable);
    nsmgr2.AddNamespace("dn",cryptoparams.m_namespace );
    //
    // Retrieve the node contents to be encrypted.
    //
    XmlNode node=dom2.SelectSingleNode(
        @"//dn:"+cryptoparams.m_encryptnode,nsmgr2);
    //
    // Encrypt the data with the client's public key.
    //
    string enc_str=SymmetricEncrypt(
        node.InnerXml,symmetricKey,symmetricIV);
    node.InnerText=enc_str;
    //
    // Return the XML to a stream and
    // copy to the networkstream.
    //
    MemoryStream encryptedstream=new MemoryStream();
    dom2.Save(encryptedstream);
    encryptedstream.Position=0;
    Copy(encryptedstream,networkstream);
}
else{
    newstream.Position=0;
    Copy(newstream,networkstream);
}
break;
    }
}
```

This code carries out the processing for both encrypting and decrypting elements of the SOAP message. *ProcessMessage* is called repeatedly with a different message stage each time. When the message stage is *BeforeDeserialize*, a SOAP message has been received but not yet deserialized into an object. This is your opportunity to decrypt the encrypted section of the message.

First it's necessary to copy the data held in the *networkstream* object to the *newstream* object. The code for the *Copy* method looks like this:

```
private void Copy(Stream fromStream, Stream toStream){
    StreamReader reader = new StreamReader(fromStream);
    StreamWriter writer = new StreamWriter(toStream);
    writer.WriteLine(reader.ReadToEnd());
    writer.Flush();
}
```

This code is very simple. It uses a *StreamReader* object and a *StreamWriter* object to copy *fromStream* to *toStream*.

Now *newstream* contains the data received by the Web method. The pointer to the action location in the stream needs to be set back to the beginning of the stream. Setting *newstream.Position* to 0 achieves this. The next three lines of code load the stream into an XML Document Object Model (DOM). Now you need to retrieve only the element that needs to be decrypted. To be able to use the DOM's *SelectSingleNode* method, the namespace for the SOAP message needs to be added to the DOM. You do so by creating an *XmlNamespaceManager* linked to the DOM that you're using and then adding the necessary namespace using the *AddNamespace* method. The necessary namespace is provided as a parameter of the *CryptoExtension* attribute. Within the *CryptoExtension* code, the value is held in the *cryptoparams.m_namespace* property.

The following *if* structure is used to check whether data needs to be either decrypted or encrypted. The values being tested are *cryptoparams.m_encryptnode* and *cryptoparams.m_decryptnode*. As with the *cryptoparams.m_namespace* property, these values are provided with the *CryptoExtension* attribute. If either encryption or decryption is necessary, a symmetric key, asymmetrically encrypted with the server's public key, should be contained within a SOAP header element named *RSAHeader*. The code searches for this node, makes sure the node is not null, and then uses the *AsymmetricDecrypt* method twice to decrypt the symmetric key and IV. It's important to note that even if only data within the SOAP response is to be encrypted, this section of code runs to get hold of the symmetric key and IV that will be used to encrypt the selected element of the SOAP response.

The remainder of the code in the *BeforeDeserialize* section of the *Process-Message* method deals with decrypting an element of the inbound SOAP request. First the XML node that contains the encrypted data is retrieved. The contents of this node are decrypted using the *SymmetricDecrypt* method. The encrypted data in the XML node is then replaced by the decrypted data. The remainder of the code returns the XML document back into a stream. The document is saved to a memory stream called *decryptedstream*. The *decryptedstream* stream needs to be copied to the *newstream* object, not the *networkstream* object, because it no longer has any use in this SOAP request. The *newstream* object length is set to 0, effectively clearing the stream, and then *decryptedstream* is copied to *newstream*.

The data that was encrypted in the SOAP request is now decrypted. The SOAP message is now deserialized into an object by the .NET Framework as normal.

Data that needs to be encrypted for a SNAP response, outbound to a client, is dealt with in the *ProcessMessage* method when the *SoapMessageStage* is *AfterSerialize*. Note that when the *ProcessMessage* method is at the *AfterSerialize* stage, the SOAP message is contained in *newstream*, not *networkstream*. You should process the contents of *newstream* and then copy the resulting stream into *networkstream* to get the response sent across the network.

Processing begins by setting the position of *newstream* to 0. Then the code checks to see whether *m_encryptnode* is not null, indicating that an element of the outbound SOAP message should be encrypted. The rest of the code is very similar to the code that decrypted an inbound element. The stream is loaded into an XML DOM, the node to encrypt is found, the contents are encrypted using symmetric encryption, and the resulting string is placed back into the DOM. Finally the XML is saved back to the stream and then copied to the *networkstream* object.

If you scroll through the ServerCrypto.cs file, you'll also see the four methods in the *CryptoExtension* class that deal with encrypting and decrypting data: *AsymmetricEncrypt*, *AsymmetricDecrypt*, *SymmetricEncrypt*, and *SymmetricDecrypt*. Three other classes exist in the ServerCrypto.cs file: *CryptoExtensionAttribute*, *CryptoParams*, and *RSAHeader*. The *CryptoExtensionAttribute* class inherits from *SoapExtensionAttribute* and allows the Web method that needs to either receive or send encrypted data to use the *CryptoExtension* class. The *SoapExtensionAttribute* class was discussed earlier in this chapter. The *Crypto-Params* class is used to hold the three parameters provided in the *Crypto-Extension* attribute. These parameters are received as part of the *CryptoExtensionAttribute* constructor. Placing the three parameters into a single object allows the object to be passed easily using the *CryptoExtension* class's

GetInitializer and *Initialize* methods. The *RSAHeader* class defines the contents of the optional SOAP header. This header contains the asymmetrically encrypted symmetric key and IV.

Now that we've examined the changes to the Web service to enable the encryption, we need to examine the changes necessary with the client. Remember that this client is an ASP.NET Web application, not a Windows application. This client application allows the user to enter a name and address, select a satellite configuration, and then submit the order. The client calls the Web services of two, theoretically remote Web services of Install Company1 and Install Company2. If one of the two installation companies covers the postal code specified by the user, the user is able to confirm the order. Otherwise, the user is informed that the order can't be completed.

You can open the secured version of the Satellite Installation Web site application from Microsoft Press\XMLWSOrg\Chapter6\Encryption\Satellite-Site\SatelliteSite.sln. The following code shows the contents of the new, secured OrderPage.aspx.cs file. As before, each line of code added to the original solution from Chapter 5 is in boldface.

```
private void Button1_Click(object sender, System.EventArgs e) {
    if (Page.IsValid){
        Session["FirstName"]=txtFirstName.Text;
        Session["LastName"]=txtLastName.Text;
        Session["Address1"]=txtAddress1.Text;
        Session["Address2"]=txtAddress2.Text;
        Session["City"]=txtCity.Text;
        Session["State"]=lstState.SelectedItem.Text;
        Session["ZipCOde"]=txtZipCode.Text;
        if (RadioButton1.Checked){
            Session["OrderType"]="A";
        }
        else if (RadioButton2.Checked){
            Session["OrderType"]="B";
        }
        else{
            Session["OrderType"]="C";
        }
        localhost.customerinfo CustInfo=new localhost.customerinfo();
        CustInfo.firstname=txtFirstName.Text;
        CustInfo.lastname=txtLastName.Text;
        CustInfo.address1 =txtAddress1.Text;
        CustInfo.address2=txtAddress2.Text;
        CustInfo.city=txtCity.Text;
        CustInfo.state=lstState.SelectedItem.Text;
        CustInfo.zipcode=txtZipCode.Text;
        CustInfo.custref="Fabrikam";
```

```
Application.Lock();
int ord;
if (Application["OrderRef"]==null){
    Application["OrderRef"]=1;
    ord=1;
}
else{
    ord=(int)Application["OrderRef"];
    ord++;
    Application["OrderRef"]=ord;
}
CustInfo.orderref=ord.ToString();
Session["OrderRef"]=ord;
Application.UnLock();
localhost.Install installWS=new localhost.Install();
String[] WebServiceURLs=new String[2];
WebServiceURLs[0]="http://localhost/XMLWSOrg/Chapter6/"+
    "Encryption/InstallCompany2/Service1.asmx";
WebServiceURLs[1]="http://localhost/XMLWSOrg/Chapter6/"+
    "Encryption/InstallCompany1/Install.asmx";
bool ok=false;
for(int p=0;p<2;p++){
    installWS.Url=WebServiceURLs[p];
    //
    // To enable the security of the data going to the server,
    // first get the server's public key.
    //
    WebForm1.ServerPublicKey=installWS.GetPublicKey();

    RijndaelManaged RMCrypto=new RijndaelManaged();
    WebForm1.SymmetricKey=RMCrypto.Key;
    WebForm1.SymmetricIV=RMCrypto.IV;

    localhost.RSAHeader rsaheader=new localhost.RSAHeader();
    rsaheader.EncryptedSymmetricKey=CryptoExtension.
        AsymmetricEncrypt(RMCrypto.Key,ServerPublicKey);
    rsaheader.EncryptedSymmetricIV=CryptoExtension.
        AsymmetricEncrypt(RMCrypto.IV,ServerPublicKey);
    installWS.RSAHeaderValue=rsaheader;
    localhost.AppointmentInfo ai=installWS.GetAppointment
        (CustInfo,(string)Session["OrderType"]);
    if (ai.Accepted){
        Session["Appointment"]=ai.AppointmentDateTime;
        Session["InstallCompany"]=ai.CompanyName;
        Session["InstallURL"]=WebServiceURLs[p];
        ok=true;
        break;
    }
```

```
        }
        if (ok){
            Page.Response.Redirect("ConfirmOrder.aspx");
        }
        else{
            Page.Response.Redirect("RejectOrder.aspx");
        }
    }
}
```

Only seven statements have been added to the OrderPage.aspx.cs file. These seven statements get the public key from the remote Web service, generate a symmetric key and IV, encrypt the symmetric key and IV with the asymmetric public key, and then place the encrypted key and IV into the object that represents the SOAP header.

In the Web service, an attribute was used on the Web method to indicate the need to either decrypt the inbound data or encrypt the outbound data. However, in the client application, no additional attributes have been added to the OrderPage.aspx.cs file. On the client side, the method that requires the attribute is contained in the proxy class generated when the Web service reference is added to the file. If you have the solution open in Visual Studio .NET 2003, on the Project menu, click Show All Files. In the Solution Explorer window, expand Web References, expand localhost, and then expand Reference.map. Now double-click the Reference.cs file. The definition of the *GetAppointment* method looks like this:

```
[System.Web.Services.Protocols.SoapHeaderAttribute
("RSAHeaderValue", Required=false)]
[System.Web.Services.Protocols.SoapDocumentMethodAttribute
    ("http://fabrikam.com/XMLWSOrg/GetAppointment",
    RequestNamespace="http://fabrikam.com/XMLWSOrg",
    ResponseNamespace="http://fabrikam.com/XMLWSOrg",
    Use=System.Web.Services.Description.SoapBindingUse.Literal,
    ParameterStyle=System.Web.Services.Protocols.
        SoapParameterStyle.Wrapped)]
[CryptoExtension("cust","AppointmentDateTime",
    "http://fabrikam.com/XMLWSOrg")]
public AppointmentInfo GetAppointment(customerinfo cust, string ordertype) {
    object[] results = this.Invoke("GetAppointment", new object[] {
        cust, ordertype});
    return ((AppointmentInfo)(results[0]));
}
```

All this code except the line shown in boldface is provided by the proxy class generator when the Web service is referenced within Visual Studio .NET 2003. The line of code in boldface has to be added to bind the encryption/

decryption functionality of the *CryptoExtension* class. If you needed to update this Web reference, you would have to add this line back into the file.

That leaves one file left to examine, the ClientCrypto.cs file. This file contains the *CryptoExtension* class and supporting classes. At first glance, you might be tempted to say that the ClientCrypto.cs file is the same as the ServerCrypto.cs file shown earlier. The two files are very similar; most of the processing is identical. The slight difference between the two has to do with the retrieval of the symmetric key and IV. For the client-side code, the symmetric key and IV are generated and held locally, so they're available to encrypt or decrypt as necessary. For the server-side code, the symmetric key and IV have to be extracted from the SOAP header that should have been sent with the request. Once extracted, the key and the IV have to be decrypted using the server's asymmetric private key.

To test that this connection does secure the data, it's worthwhile to look at the SOAP messages that are exchanged between the client and the server. The SOAP messages were monitored using the SOAP Toolkit 3 Trace utility. You can find more information on the Trace utility in Chapter 1; however, there is a slight difference in the procedure. This time you should add the port address of 8080 to the URLs held in the *WebServiceURLs* array and not the URL specified in the Reference.cs file because this URL is superseded by the URL held in the array at run time. The Satellite Installation Web site page that starts off the transaction is shown in Figure 6-4.

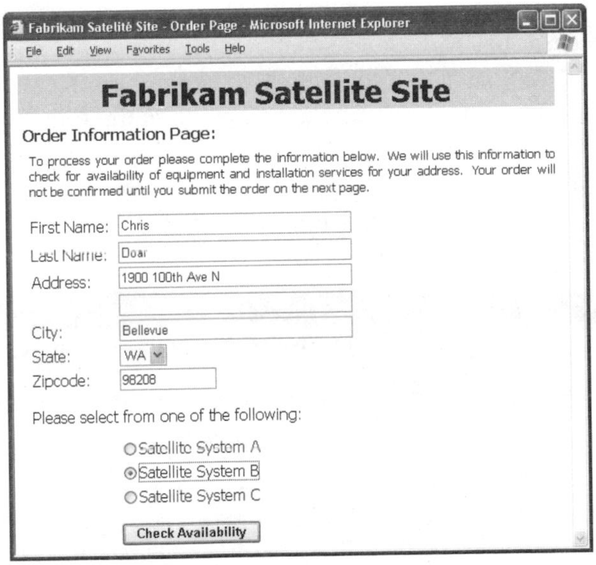

Figure 6-4   The Satellite Installation Web site order information page

The following SOAP message is the request from the client to the server for the server's public asymmetric key:

```
<?xml version="1.0" encoding="utf-8"?>
<soap:Envelope xmlns:soap="http://schemas.xmlsoap.org/soap/envelope/"
  xmlns:xsi="http://www.w3.org/2001/XMLSchema-instance"
  xmlns:xsd="http://www.w3.org/2001/XMLSchema">
  <soap:Body>
    <GetPublicKey xmlns="http://fabrikam.com/XMLWSOrg" />
  </soap:Body>
</soap:Envelope>
```

The response from the server contains the server's public key.

```
<?xml version="1.0" encoding="utf-8"?>
<soap:Envelope xmlns:soap="http://schemas.xmlsoap.org/soap/envelope/"
xmlns:xsi="http://www.w3.org/2001/XMLSchema-instance" xmlns:xsd="http://
www.w3.org/2001/XMLSchema">
  <soap:Body>
    <GetPublicKeyResponse xmlns="http://fabrikam.com/XMLWSOrg">
      <GetPublicKeyResult><RSAKeyValue><Modulus>tWlDAgfsFTZpk
        BvccU7jeA2amF0O8ZEM2dT9RpMDm+NnefU87QtxPb/ynXTzbnzDconw3fbJkPi2Z
        huce65twXvyFGhB2WF9/zo2exl9PctuievUGZJ36192nUU1AGLMaJWe92sJ1Amp0O
        5CITCL33pdsVApF70E2iJtPdsGw6s=</Modulus><Exponent>
        AQAB</Exponent></RSAKeyValue></GetPublicKeyResult>
    </GetPublicKeyResponse>
  </soap:Body>
</soap:Envelope>
```

Now that the client has the server's public key, the actual call to the *Get-Appointment* method that contains the sensitive personal information can be made. Notice that the personal information is encrypted in the following message:

```
<?xml version="1.0" encoding="utf-8"?>
<soap:Envelope xmlns:soap="http://schemas.xmlsoap.org/soap/envelope/"
  xmlns:xsi="http://www.w3.org/2001/XMLSchema-instance"
  xmlns:xsd="http://www.w3.org/2001/XMLSchema">
  <soap:Header>
    <RSAHeader xmlns="http://fabrikam.com/XMLWSOrg">
      <EncryptedSymmetricKey>BkqAhRC8UkFYuxbjOcGch/ahaqGyu+nCg06h3Bm
        ObewG9oHlfnvPZlL48zwoiyg4rzoYyYma8kAzMpcZXkdBr0aotBxzW9Wldslx
        nRooynFoCzuNypkc6Zs8ThnaYTMYSlvcm+euHS8bwAXSrSHaw7WlaCUcrx2as
        FsObON1Q04=
      </EncryptedSymmetricKey>
      <EncryptedSymmetricIV>VcHjIIlYnP48CuQyz9wYs5iZ101WiZFlmrV7oERY
        2ml9u0opoAjUxN1s0RMoV5JxbqFEcACUt47wRuhtyW9M2X4VSO0JtWd9htuhzJ
        Dzu04a4n2XSHwRcs0OkGsF+g3QVLz4vl10XZzJek6INwPxRWrfdQcHKsHYmNCwh
        mGnUDc=
      </EncryptedSymmetricIV>
    </RSAHeader>
```

```
    </RSAHeader>
  </soap:Header>
  <soap:Body>
    <GetAppointment xmlns="http://fabrikam.com/XMLWSOrg">
      <cust>1BRURdyR2oMpsB06mB8Vi6AncKLvoQ7ckVOJCtybsovA8t21AFmupy
+8QavyQlgCjr3wrQyZMxxLZYKvb9WL80tzXmWX2PSxQT02MNzidQeRyRSyE9uBybAs
sRnGmtytObL0YkiRr6p7buqp7JwDjNkucRL9fjuXTG1rSPdkaHTsa2bTS6wHsARlz0
h2XNCv6T9oewsPCUofbMZEU63aIoKGHavj9nRIhY4ym2/+go7pSpjaOjbOfOpyirIV
BsO6JvagiZj/8IVEF39weh8ZqqtnrxEh/oEVbMvFYP5uHwyQ1bahDc7prahTCJ7Sj/
LwVELuqgzPbfO1UA9unVV1VuSsfMXI+uceMrlkKHASX0kEO1TTXSmhW5VDjm+1M92q
7bqmylc72nrSXldTYEywQ9ZhkjcShTvCEqzlKtyDcDCtdFrb+k9w3/wELzHhN+mcuJ
A7L5fK+RdV655BfPx3+dBa7yYIsg51rLyencNYmJPzLPYYDiJ4AqbntCeaETWI/5jU
hoCySqzOAsJ2i9ni471QR5E+A9tjmYV7OIeLPXCEMb41m6SqwbX1p+tOblCn7/DrBC
nZdlnjHRG5/hYp6IRSD2wQf78jg1AC8buDg7bBrNWJQgXCX01n4ncR/3Zzi+9nBqEc
uLhqMyE9zDwzPnolVcjCQZEjxFBxIQaFrAZq4xFjDH2SHUJGishxhYs0PmAamXZuPJ
44K30IpHmyMx+VYNiGmnfYyyT3wZW0tzG717tHEYNqJrD4oZ1pY53hNOna7g0AaGL6
MsjHMDi0ci/qwdqEVHaiaT5kD+4u40Q4c+zRa3exZSktbGCoBWLVjishkz187y+rkh
8e4D3J6abSsCbrjjeW+nT59D+qmYzm/TcvO6bpfKcfpGBFmYX0d881d/xpQ8zeLeKL
k2BdemJczrq6elaeqymeUKYqdnKGD01He131e3vHoOONcCrFNbB7TE0tN9U+pUQ9/5
bRDKNs3eAQcaJZQ46JOq2TgFit4PtZEYmruOwVz98PbGNcgvrA56G1BmzwdDMICXq2
e3jmh1R/rit4abTQN14q5DRKEU2ptvHufSBm/K3z7m+4NDyydmAOidUn+SksyvFPMc
t1qdQGghH0VGNTje9oyGLuSEhmkHjRkohTinTOyVEkS3zQZSCyUxuGEBtifEDvC7HM
n9VTWmU/HTfyrCbEDVJrLfllx7kBpCHJuH4Kkx7r81I/1M8jBl+pC1r3gefLlaLVxp
/30YNPgCv+JpGWts8vrhYKKBJptuGjJMgB2cywyU1jsSpCNScAnCW38h+B0JPuZHnO
39FVHh1pbCNBzck4x0r2v36CCqel9P6JdIr1CaxjaulSXu1avXo63ftaSoo3K0Yhdq
VqGPnVFJtRQvDT2AkI0aMvaT3g6oszeiQ4FieuB9Tt978aSMSD3vThARLGty9wGI2P
OuyS2mQAOK1Uvr65d7ROG71K8v1EjU9ERq7G3DuttWr0Ad01cYgWyS1CJgJHOs4dnY
mEQGw53k8J6sX135IYpiqM/6BPfz1RmKThJRSUR80I88GCEuZRqvepuoqsGy3yVxti
YrD3K3iJeg8fphJllKtB70NjL2hXHpw3J61sMct0kYr81tb76pcruS7S3w1V6SZkhK
viBe+P2V5jLmsrIUjGkntZHeTsk62nyDX2DWJMZM67YwEqlIABvHQAoR61zl61vwcC
ISKDfR2ymJucg42yUU5QyDl7</cust>
      <ordertype>B</ordertype>
    </GetAppointment>
  </soap:Body>
</soap:Envelope>
```

Notice the SOAP header in the SOAP message. The SOAP header contains the encrypted symmetric key created by the client to encrypt the data in the SOAP body. Also notice that not all of the SOAP body is encrypted, only the *cust* element. The *ordertype* element is clearly visible. Using SOAP messages in a remote procedure call (RPC) request/response system and leaving some of the message unencrypted might not be that important. However, if your SOAP message is destined to pass through a number of services on its journey, the ability for some of the data to be secure while other parts are nonsecure is more useful. This ability to "route" a SOAP message through a number of nodes is being written into the emerging SOAP standards.

The final SOAP response, shown here, contains the appointment information if the customer's address falls into the coverage area of the installation company:

```xml
<?xml version="1.0" encoding="utf-8"?>
<soap:Envelope xmlns:soap="http://schemas.xmlsoap.org/soap/envelope/"
  xmlns:xsi="http://www.w3.org/2001/XMLSchema-instance"
  xmlns:xsd="http://www.w3.org/2001/XMLSchema">
  <soap:Body>
    <GetAppointmentResponse xmlns="http://fabrikam.com/XMLWSOrg">
      <GetAppointmentResult>
        <Accepted>true</Accepted>
        <AppointmentDateTime>LAIXlnOPLoteFYvBaMrX2gJijJHitwja9lW0uM
          glFfndvOafCyjukzlvhRegeruBmun01GIgfInVGgzvIVIRVqD9MvkN5Hb
          NeJh3ZLF+yxg=
        </AppointmentDateTime>
        <CompanyName>Install Company 2</CompanyName>
      </GetAppointmentResult>
    </GetAppointmentResponse>
  </soap:Body>
</soap:Envelope>
```

Once the SOAP messages have been exchanged, the results are displayed to the client in the Satellite Installation Web site application, as shown in Figure 6-5.

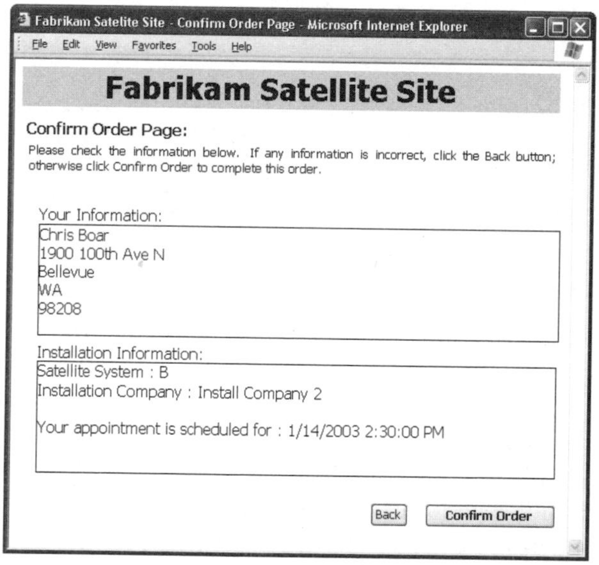

Figure 6-5   The Satellite Installation Web site Confirm Order page

The code contained in the ServerCrypto.cs and ClientCrypto.cs files is designed to encrypt and decrypt a single element within the SOAP message. You might need to encrypt multiple elements. The concepts do not change; you would need to manipulate the code a little to meet your needs. The final topic we'll discuss in this chapter is the issue of ensuring that the data you received actually came from who you think it did. This verification will not always be needed, but in the encrypted example earlier, anyone can get the server's public key, encrypt some data with it, and then supply that data to the server. It's possible that a message sent from one of your trading partners could have been swapped for a different message. The contents of the original message will be secure, but the encryption does not guarantee that the message you receive is the one that was sent. To ensure data integrity, you need some sort of signature.

Ensuring the Integrity of Data Exchanged

Signatures depend on asymmetric encryption and decryption. To ensure that data originated from a particular trading partner, your trading partner could encrypt the data with a private key and then send you the encrypted data along with the data itself. If you use the trading partner's public key to successfully decrypt the data and the decrypted data matches the unencrypted data sent from the partner, you know the data originated from your trading partner and has not been tampered with over the network.

In reality, this system fails if the size of the data exceeds the size of data that can be encrypted with the asymmetric algorithm. Remember that the size of the data is related to the size of the key used in the algorithm. What you need to do is generate something that represents the data but is small enough to be asymmetrically encrypted, which is accomplished using hashing algorithms.

Introducing Hash Algorithms

A hash algorithm generates a value of fixed size from a large block of data. It is statistically unlikely that two different blocks of data will produce the same hash value. Small changes to the original data make large changes to the hash value. Now that you have the hash value, it can be encrypted with a private key and sent with the data as the signature. Encrypting only the hash value involves less processing than encrypting the entire data block.

The .NET Framework makes generating a signature and verifying a signature very straightforward. The following code returns a byte array containing the signed hash value, which is the signature.

```
public byte[] GenerateSignature(Stream inputStream,string private_key){
    RSACryptoServiceProvider rsa=new RSACryptoServiceProvider();
    rsa.FromXmlString(private_key);
    return rsa.SignData(inputStream,new SHA1CryptoServiceProvider());
}
```

Notice the *SHA1CryptoServiceProvider* class specified on the last line. This specification informs the *SignData* method which .NET-supplied hash algorithm to use. The following code uses the *VerifyData* method of the *RSACryptoServiceProvider* class to verify a signature against some data:

```
public bool VerifySignature(Stream inputStream,
    byte[] signature,string public_key){
    RSACryptoServiceProvider rsa=new RSACryptoServiceProvider();
    rsa.FromXmlString(public_key);
    byte[] buffer=new Byte[inputStream.Length];
    inputStream.Position=0;
    inputStream.Read(buffer,0,(int)inputStream.Length);
    return rsa.VerifyData(buffer,new
        SHA1CryptoServiceProvider(),signature);
}
```

The following code pulls together the previous two procedures:

```
RSACryptoServiceProvider rsa=new RSACryptoServiceProvider();
string private_key=rsa.ToXmlString(true);
string public_key=rsa.ToXmlString(false);
MemoryStream ms=new MemoryStream();
StreamWriter sw=new StreamWriter(ms);
sw.Write("This is test data.");
sw.Flush();
ms.Position=0;

byte[] signature=GenerateSignature(ms,private_key);

if (VerifySignature(ms,signature,public_key)){
    MessageBox.Show("Signature verifies the data.");
}
else {
    MessageBox.Show("Signature does not verify the data!");
}
```

In all the cryptographic code in this chapter, certificates have not been used. A digital certificate contains the subject's public key and information about who issued the digital certificate. If you trust the issuer of the digital certificate, you can use the digital certificate to encrypt and decrypt data and to verify signatures. Windows has a cryptographic store where certificates are held. Some of these certificates will be your own, so they will contain both a private and public key; other certificates contain only a public key.

> **Note** Web Services Enhancements 1 for Microsoft .NET includes support for WS-Security, WS-Routing (and WS-Referral), DIME, and WS-Attachments. However, at the time of this writing, support for these additions to the basic SOAP standard in other toolsets is minimal. When more Web service toolsets include support for this new functionality, you should definitely consider using them because they should reduce the overall amount of coding you have to do.

In version 1.1 of the .NET Framework, access to the cryptographic store was not provided. It's possible to access the store using unmanaged code such as CAPICOM (intended for Microsoft Visual Basic or Visual Basic Scripting Edition) or CryptoAPI (intended for C++ developers). In December 2002, Microsoft released Web Services Enhancements 1 for Microsoft .NET, which is available at *http://msdn.microsoft.com/webservices/building/wse/default.aspx*. This software provides additional advanced Web service functionality, including classes that can read certificates, and therefore keys, from the cryptographic stores held on the local machine. If you need to implement security using keys from digital certificates, I recommend that you download and install this software and study the provided help and samples.

Extra Credit

You can do your extra credit for this chapter at two levels. For the first level, draw a diagram that includes a client and a server and the flow of information between the client and the server to both encrypt the data that moves from the client to the server and to sign that data. Without giving the solution away, this process will involve the exchange of public keys between the client and the server.

For the second level, if you want to go further, implement the solution you designed in level 1. You should be able to leverage a considerable amount of the code in the ServerCrypto.cs and ClientCrypto.cs files. However, do not underestimate this task. If you get it all working, you have proven your skills with both Web services and cryptography.

Summary

This chapter covered a great deal. First it covered some basic cryptographic information, including symmetric and asymmetric encryption. It looked at symmetric keys and IVs. It covered the relationship between and use of public and private key pairs used in asymmetric encryption. This chapter also covered the .NET Framework classes that support cryptography.

The chapter then moved on to authentication and authorization. Authentication is another area in which digital certificates can be used to prove identities.

During the discussion of encryption, this chapter introduced the *SoapExtension* class and its *SoapExtensionAttribute* supporting class. You should understand that the *SoapExtension* class provides you with access to the data at one of four stages of processing.

Finally the chapter introduced data integrity and signatures, including the use of hash algorithms to reduce the size of the data to be encrypted with the sender's private key. The SOAP messages produced by the code in this chapter utilize standard public encryption algorithms. Your trading partners should be able to decrypt your messages as long as they have the correct keys and implementations of the same algorithms you used to encrypt the data.

7

Monitoring, Scaling, and the Future

In this final chapter, we look at monitoring your XML-based Web services, how to scale them, and, finally, where this technology is going. You need to think about what you can do in your Web services to provide data to those who will manage the servers on which your service will eventually run. If your Web service will end up supporting large numbers of connections, you need to consider how to scale your service. Web services are a young and rapidly changing technology. Even during the writing of this book, new functionality was being added to SOAP. As support for these new standards grows, you might want to consider leveraging this new functionality.

Monitoring Your Web Services

You should monitor your Web services during development and once they're deployed into a live environment. Monitoring your service will help you spot any performance or faults at an early stage.

ASP.NET offers out-of-the-box performance data that can be viewed from the Perfmon.exe performance-monitoring tool. You can start Perfmon.exe by opening Control Panel, Administrative Tools, and then double-clicking Performance. The Performance console includes two snap-ins, System Monitor and Performance Logs And Alerts. You can select Help Topics from the Help menu to get detailed information on using this tool. ASP.NET supports global system performance counters and application performance counters. You can use application performance counters to monitor the performance of a specific ASP.NET application. You might also notice an instance named *__Total__* in the performance-monitoring tool, which aggregates counter values for all applications on a Web server.

There are 12 performance counters within the ASP.NET system group and 46 performance counters within the ASP.NET application group. I considered listing these counters here, but I want to focus instead on how you as a developer provide your own custom performance counters. For more information on these counters, I strongly recommend the article "ASP.NET Performance Monitoring, and When to Alert Administrators" written by Thomas Marquardt (Microsoft Corporation, February 2003) available from MSDN at *http://msdn.microsoft.com/library/default.asp?url=/library/en-us/dnaspp/html /monitor_perf.asp.*

Implementing Custom Performance Counters

To use custom performance counters, you first have to create the custom counters and then update them.

Creating Custom Performance Counters

Within the *System.Diagnostics* namespace are a number of classes that provide you with an interface to the Microsoft Windows system performance counters. Using these classes, you can not only read the values from the counters, but also create new counter groups and counters. We'll use the following four classes:

- ***PerformanceCounterCategory.***   Defines a category of performance counters.

- ***CounterCreationData.***   Define the counter type, name, and help string for a new counter. Think of this class as a description of the new counter.

- ***CounterCreationDataCollection.***   A collection of *CounterCreation-Data* objects. Think of this class as instructions to create new counters.

- ***PerformanceCounter.***   An instance of a performance counter held on the system.

Using these classes, you can create and update your own performance counters from within your Web service.

The first step is to create a new performance category and the counters you want to use within it. However, the security context in which the Web service runs does not by default have enough permission to create new performance categories or counters. It does, however, have enough permission to update custom performance objects that already exist. You could solve this problem by changing the security context for the service, but doing so is dangerous. The security level for the Web service has been set to minimize risks, and there's an easier way around the problem. The solution is to set up the performance categories and counters when the Web service is deployed. This way, they are set up within the security context of the logged-on user, hopefully an administrator of the machine. The following code is a simple console-based setup application that adds a performance category and two counters:

```
using System;
using System.Diagnostics;

namespace SetupPWSCounters
{
    /// <summary>
    /// Summary description for Class1.
    /// </summary>
    class Class1
    {
        /// <summary>
        /// The main entry point for the application.
        /// </summary>
        [STAThread]
        static void Main(string[] args)
        {
            if (args.Length>0 && args[0]=="/D" | args[0]=="/d"){
                if (PerformanceCounterCategory.Exists
                    ("PerformanceWebService")){
                    PerformanceCounterCategory.Delete
                        ("PerformanceWebService");
                    Console.WriteLine("PerformanceWebService "+
                        "counters deleted.");
                }
            }
            else{
                if (!PerformanceCounterCategory.Exists
                    ("PerformanceWebService")){
                    CounterCreationDataCollection pCounters=
                        new CounterCreationDataCollection();
                    CounterCreationData processedCounter=
                        new CounterCreationData("Processed",
                        "Count of the number of times the Test "+
                        "Web method has been called",
                        PerformanceCounterType.NumberOfItems32);
                    pCounters.Add(processedCounter);
                    CounterCreationData processedPerSec=
```

```
                new CounterCreationData("Processed Per Sec",
                    "Processed per second",
                    PerformanceCounterType.RateOfCountsPerSecond32);
                pCounters.Add(processedPerSec);
                PerformanceCounterCategory.Create
                    ("PerformanceWebService","Performance "+
                        "Web Service",pCounters);
                Console.WriteLine("Configuration complete,"+
                    " performance counters created.");
            }
            else{
                Console.WriteLine("Configuration complete "+
                    "(no changes necessary).");
            }
        }
        Console.WriteLine("Press a key to continue...");
        Console.ReadLine();
    }
}
}
```

From this book's sample files, you can open this solution at Microsoft Press\XMLWSOrg\Chapter7\SetupPWSCounters.sln. This code allows for an installation and an uninstallation by adding a */d* parameter to the command line. The code uses the *Exists* static method of the *PerformanceCounterCategory* class to check if the category has already been created. If the category does not exist, an instance of the *CounterCreationDataCollection* class is created. Each performance counter is created using a *CounterCreationData* class instance. The constructor for this class needs the name of the counter, a description of the counter, and the type of the counter.

There are 28 different performance counter types. This code sample uses the *NumberOfItems32* and *RateOfCountsPerSecond32* types. *NumberOfItems32* is a simple counter. If you increment this counter, the count will appear in the Perfmon application. *RateOfCountsPerSecond32* converts the count information you update to the counter into a count-per-second figure that's then available to the Perfmon application. Other counter types track timing and averages.

After each *CounterCreationData* instance is created, it's added to *CounterCreationDataCollection*. Finally the *Create* static method of the *PerformanceCounterCategory* class is used to add the new category and its counters. The *Create* method needs the new category name, a description of the category, and the *CounterCreationDataCollection* instance.

After you have run this setup routine, you can see the new category named *PerformanceWebService* in the Perfmon's Add Counters window, as shown in Figure 7-1. To display this window, right-click the Perfmon's details pane and click Add Counters. All that's left to do now is update these counters from a Web service.

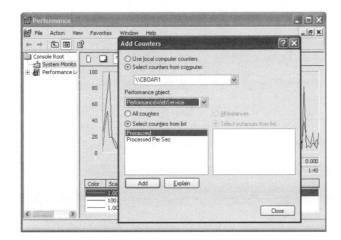

Figure 7-1   The Perfmon's Add Counters window displaying the new performance category

Updating Custom Performance Counters

Now that the performance category and counters are created, updating them is very simple. The following code is from the PerformanceWebService that you can open from Microsoft Press\XMLWSOrg\Chapter7\PerformanceWeb-Service\PerformanceWebService.sln:

```
[WebMethod]
public string Test(int val)
{
    PerformanceCounter processedCounter=new PerformanceCounter(
        "PerformanceWebService","Processed",false);
    PerformanceCounter processedRateCounter=new PerformanceCounter(
        "PerformanceWebService","Processed Per Sec",false);
    processedCounter.IncrementBy(val);
    processedRateCounter.Increment();
    return "Test Result";
}
```

I have kept this Web service deliberately short and simple. Make sure that you reference the *System.Diagnostics* namespace and then create an instance of the *PerformanceCounter* class. The constructor accepts the name of the performance category (created by the setup routine), the name of the actual counter within that category, and a Boolean value indicating whether the counter should be opened read-only. In this case, we need to be able to update the counters, so the value is *false*.

There are two methods and one property of direct interest available on the *PerformanceCounter* object.

- *Increment* **method.** Increments the counter by 1.

- *IncrementBy(value)* **method.** Increments the counter by the value passed as a parameter.

- *RawValue* **property.** Sets the counter to a specific value.

Within the sample files, I have provided a simple test client that makes a number of calls to the PerformanceWebService, which allows you to watch the counters change in the Perfmon application. The code is at Microsoft Press\XML-WSOrg\Chapter7\PerformanceClient\PerformanceClient.sln. First open Perfmon, and configure a graph with one or both of the new performance counters. Now run the performance client, click the Start button in the client application, and watch the counters change. You should see something like Figure 7-2.

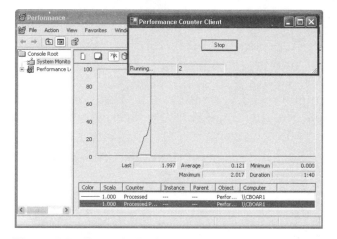

Figure 7-2 Example Perfmon output displaying the PerformanceWeb-Service test counters

Before we leave performance counters, we should give a little thought to exactly what type of information you might want to make available by creating a custom performance counter. This information will vary from Web service to Web service, but the following kinds of counters are worth considering:

- **Data errors.** You should try to trap bad data as much as possible within your code rather than using exceptions, which are not as efficient. For example, if your Web service needs to divide one value by another, you should check for the possibility of a divide-by-zero error. This error might then increment an error counter or perhaps even a specific divide-by-zero error counter.

- **Successful transactions.** In your code, you can define what a successful transaction looks like. This type of information is useful to a support person who monitors a Web service over a period of time. Once trends in this metric have been established, changes in the figures can warn of a problem.

- **Transaction types.** If your Web service supports authenticated and anonymous requests, you could provide counters to track how many of each type of connection you receive.

- **The average value of a transaction.** This type of counter is less useful to a support person but might be interesting to a business person.

- **Security issues.** These are similar to error counters, but I think it's good to call them out separately. An example of a security counter would be in a Web service where you have implemented a custom authentication mechanism, perhaps using user IDs and passwords stored in a database table. You should count each successful and unsuccessful authentication attempt because a spike in failed authentications might indicate that someone is trying to hack into your Web service.

Once you've designed and implemented your performance counters, make sure that you document them. After all, you might not be monitoring your Web service, but someone else should be.

The information retrieved from counting failed SOAP authentications with a performance counter object is a good example of information that should also be written to the event log, as discussed in the next section.

Writing to the Application Event Log

The Windows event log is a great place to write significant event information. These events might be errors, authentication events, configuration changes, or any event that would be useful to someone supporting your Web service. If you consider the encryption sample code within the satellite installation company's Web service in Chapter 6, it would be sensible to trap the error raised if the data can't be decrypted with the private key and to write a suitable message to the event log. An error of this sort might indicate that someone is attempting to alter the data.

Writing to the event log takes two steps. The first step is to create an event log source.

```
if(!EventLog.SourceExists("PerformanceWebService")){
    EventLog.CreateEventSource("PerformanceWebService","Application");
}
```

As with the creation of the performance category and counters, creating an event log source can't be accomplished in the default security context of the Web service, so it's best done within a setup program. Once the source is created, the Web service can use that source and add event log entries.

```
EventLog.WriteEntry("PerformanceWebService",
    "Received a request",
    EventLogEntryType.Information,1000);
```

The *WriteEntry* method has various forms. The one shown in this code passes in the name of the source, the text detail of the event log, the type of event log entry to create, and an event ID. Calling the preceding code creates an entry in your event log similar to the one shown in Figure 7-3.

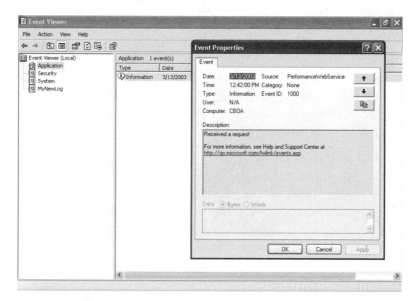

Figure 7-3   Example event log entry

As with the performance counters, you should document the event IDs that your application might write into an event log and the actions each ID might require. Otherwise, a support technician is likely to ask you what an event ID means and what to do about it.

You've been shown two methods for implementing monitoring support into your Web services. There are, of course, other methods of monitoring, from the very simple, such as writing data to flat text files, to complex custom-designed monitoring systems. Clearly, you need to look at each Web service individually, consider its uses and the risks to the business if the service fails, and then pick an appropriate level of monitoring support. I've shown you how to interface your Web service to Perfmon and the event log because these are common tools used by support personnel on Windows platforms.

Implementing Scalable Web Services

Before we examine some of the issues specific to .NET and Web services, it's worth mentioning that basic programming principles related to performance still apply here. For example, caching appropriate data can help with performance. Using locks is necessary to prevent corruption of data during updates, but they should be held for as short a time as possible. Don't use a lock if it's not necessary. You should make every effort to duplicate your production environment in your development environment. You should monitor the performance of your Web service and understand the bottlenecks.

Design your Web service interfaces carefully. It's better to provide a single method that returns a larger amount of data than multiple methods that each return an element of the data. For example, in the customer data Web service example in Chapter 2, it's more efficient to return all the information about the customer using a method such as *GetCustomerDetails* than to have a method for each different type of information, such as *GetTelephone*, *GetAddress*, and *GetCustomerName*.

To make your ASP.NET Web services scalable, consider the following issues:

- **Exceptions.**   Write your code to avoid exceptions because exceptions have a negative impact on performance. Try to write code to detect problems rather than allow them to be caught as an exception. Although this is a good principle, in practice there are times when you have no choice but to capture an exception.

- **Session state.**   If you can avoid using session state, do so. If you have to use session state, consider carefully how you set up ASP.NET to manage this data. Session data can be held in-process, out-of-process in another service, or with Microsoft SQL Server. For more information on session state options, search for the "Session State" title in the .NET Framework Developer's Guide, accessible from within Visual Studio .NET 2003 help. If it's important that session data is not lost when a server or process encounters a problem, use the SQL Server option.

- **Debug.**   Make sure that you disable debug mode when you deploy your production environment.

- **Web gardening.**   This term relates to ASP.NET being able to take advantage of multiple processors within a machine, which can have a dramatic positive effect on performance.

- *System.Web.Caching* **namespace.**   This namespace contains classes that provide data caching functionality that you can use in your Web service.

- **Output caching.**   ASP.NET allows you to specify an output caching duration for each Web method. Each output response is keyed against the input parameters and held for the duration specified. You set this cache duration using the *CacheDuration* property of the *WebMethod* attribute, as shown here:

```
[WebMethod(CacheDuration=100)]
```

Addressing Performance Problems

As with any application, if the system doesn't appear to work well, your first step should be to analyze the system to determine where the performance problems are occurring. If the performance problem is related to retrieving data from a database, you should improve the performance of data retrieval and then see how that improvement affects the system as a whole. You might want to review your code for potential performance improvements. Your next option might be to scale up the server on which the Web service is running. Your analysis of the server under load should guide you in determining whether the performance problem is an I/O, memory, or processor problem.

For example, the cryptographic functions you used in Chapter 6 are very processor-intensive. If you intend to use a lot of cryptographic functions for signing or encrypting data, you might benefit from a multiple-processor server.

The scale-out alternative to address performance problems is typically more involved. Scaling out a solution involves adding one or more servers to an existing implementation. The question then remains as to how you split the requests over the array of servers. You can use one of the following three techniques to accomplish this task:

- **Manually.**   Depending on the implementation, you might be able to inform one set of users to use one URL and another set to use a different URL. Although simple, this technique is not very clever. If one of the servers fails, the users of that server are not automatically transferred to the other server. Also, no load balancing takes place.

It's possible that all users of one server will make a request while the other server is idle.

■ **Load balancing.** Using static load balancing such as DNS round-robin or dynamic load balancing such as Microsoft's network load balancing functionality might have some impact on how you design your Web service. For example, if you're using session state within your Web service, you need to make sure that all of your servers are configured to centrally maintain that session data on a single server.

■ **Web service–based solution.** Although this option might take more work to implement, it also offers some interesting possibilities. With this solution, you build a Web service hosted on a server that receives the request from the user. Your Web service passes this request to another Web service on another machine for actual processing. The front-end Web service then passes the next request to another server, and so on. Responses received from the back-end server to the front-end server are then relayed back to the sender. The front-end server should be able to hand off requests to the back-end server quickly.

Before we leave scalability, I must mention that a number of documents in the Microsoft Windows .NET Framework documentation discuss building scalable applications and provide other specific information on ASP.NET.

Extra Credit

It's time for your final opportunity for extra credit. Using the concept of a SOAP message being passed from node to node between a starting point and an end point, consider what message paths your company might want to support. As an example to get you started, consider the dispatch of a product from Company A to Company B. The request message for the product starts at Company B. The next node is Company A. Company A could reject the request or add the message pricing information to it. The message now proceeds to the delivery company node. The delivery company logs the need for a truck to deliver the product and adds a delivery reference and time to the message. Finally the message, with all the new information, ends up back with Company B.

The Future of Web Services

The samples in this book have shown you how Web services provide serious solutions to many common IT problems. It's also true that Web services are still in their infancy. As more and more companies start to adopt this technology, situations arise in which the current standards of XML and SOAP do not provide a simple or direct solution. Developers are already working on solutions to such problems.

You can do amazing things using the Web services already available. However, as more and more companies develop solutions with Web services, the following opportunities for improvements have been identified:

- **Security.**   Companies would like an end-to-end security architecture that's easy to implement.

- **Routing.**   Companies concerned with scalability and fault tolerance want a way to define a path for a message and be able to dynamically change the message en route.

- **Reliable messaging.**   Companies with mission-critical applications need to depend on message delivery. There are different reliable message delivery options such as an at-least-once delivery or an at-most-once delivery.

- **Transactions.**   Put simply, transactions allow a consistent outcome across multiple organizations involved in a SOAP message's path. For example, if a SOAP message fails to be handled correctly by one node in a defined path, each of the previous nodes in the path is able to revert to a known state.

To address these needs, Microsoft has developed the Global XML Web Services Architecture (GXA). GXA includes a number of specifications, and more are being developed as you read this book. Many of the specifications of the GXA have been created in partnership with other organizations, including IBM. The following specification index pages exist of this writing:

- **WS-ReliableMessaging Specification Index Page.**   WS-Reliable-Messaging is a protocol for guaranteeing that messages are delivered, properly ordered, and received without duplication.

- **WS-Addressing Specification Index Page.**   Using WS-Addressing, you can indicate information in a SOAP message's header to uniquely identify a message, specify its origin and its destination, specify endpoints for errors, and describe actions required for message processing.

- **WS-Security Specification Index Page.** WS-Security allows you to provide integrity and confidentiality of a message. This specification includes WS-SecurityPolicy, WS-Trust, and WS-SecureConversation.

- **WS-Policy Specification Index Page.** This specification allows a Web service to specify its policies. It includes specifications of WS-Policy, WS-PolicyAttachment, and WS-PolicyAssertions.

- **WS-Attachments Specification Index Page.** WS-Attachments specifies how to wrap SOAP messages and attachments such as binary files into a Direct Internet Message Encapsulation (DIME) message.

- **WS-Coordination Specification Index Page.** WS-Coordination specifies an extensible framework for the definition of how applications should work together.

- **WS-Inspection Specification Index Page.** WS-Inspection specifies a method of aggregating Web service definitions to make it easier to discover Web services.

- **WS-Referral Specification Index Page.** WS-Referral specifies a protocol that allows the nodes specified in a SOAP message's path to be dynamically configured.

- **WS-Routing Specification Index Page.** WS-Routing specifies a SOAP-based protocol for routing SOAP messages over different types of transports, such as TCP and HTTP.

- **WS-Transaction Specification Index Page.** WS-Transaction specifies the coordination types that are used within the WS-Coordination specification.

These specifications are proposed standards. As such, support for them among Web service toolsets varies. At the time of this writing, Microsoft had released Web Service Enhancements 1 (WSE), service pack 1 for Microsoft .NET. This 3 MB download includes support for the WS-Security, WS-Routing, WS-Attachments, and DIME specifications. I have deliberately avoided using any of this functionality in this book's sample applications because of the limited support for these specifications in other toolsets. Given enough time and support, I'm sure these specifications will become widely adopted and should make more complex Web services possible and easier to implement.

These specifications are still subject to change, and their number will probably grow. Because of the chance of change in these specifications, I've kept the details to a minimum here and instead recommend that you consult online documentation for GXA through sites such as *http://www.msdn.microsoft.com* and *http://www.gotdotnet.com*. Each company about to implement a Web service will need to consider how many of the new specifications it can safely adopt.

Summary

This chapter looked at monitoring, scaling, and the future of Web services. Providing the support necessary to monitor your Web services is not difficult. In fact, more effort is required to plan the right performance counter to be monitored than is required for the actual task of implementing the design. Although they're not the only methods to enable monitoring, using Perfmon counters and event log entries is both simple and effective.

Monitoring your Web service is the first step to understanding its performance and what steps you might need to take to scale it. Before making any hardware or software changes, you need to understand what's causing the problem. Otherwise, you waste time and money randomly hunting for that fix that cures the performance issue.

Although Web service technology is evolving, you should not be deterred from reaping the benefits of Web services today. As the new specifications become firmer and their support with different toolsets grows, you can start to use the new specifications. Whatever the specification, it's the abstraction provided that solves so many common integration problems.

In the space of seven chapters, you've been taken from an introduction to Web services to using Web services for electronic data interchange, to cryptographic functions, to a look at the future. Each chapter has focused on a specific business problem, but each chapter has also introduced some new technical aspect of Web services.

These technical aspects are not restricted to the types of business problems covered in the chapters in which they were introduced. My primary goal was to provide examples of how Web services can overcome common business problems. A secondary goal was to introduce the rich support for Web services available with the .NET Framework. You should add each technical element covered here into your arsenal of tools for solving problems. As a developer, you have many tools at hand, and it's up to you to design an appropriate solution taking into account numerous tradeoffs.

I stand in awe of both the simplicity of Web services and their potential. They represent one of those things that, when you're introduced to it and begin to understand the concepts, you say, "Why didn't we think of that before?" Make no mistake: this is not a Microsoft-specific technology, nor is it based on proprietary protocols. There's growing support for Web services from many companies. You only have to look at the recent specifications to see names such as Ariba, BEA, IBM, and Microsoft. Web services are certainly in their infancy, but even at this stage, they're an exceptionally adaptable and viable technology.

Index

Chris Boar

Chris Boar is a member of the Training and Certification group at Microsoft, where he currently focuses on planning developer training and certification products. Chris has been writing code professionally for more than 15 years. During his career Chris has worked in the IT departments of several large manufacturing companies, as a software developer, and as a Microsoft Certified Trainer for various training and consulting firms.

The manuscript for this book was prepared and galleyed using Microsoft Word. Pages were composed by Microsoft Press using Adobe FrameMaker+SGML for Windows, with text in Garamond and display type in Helvetica Condensed. Composed pages were delivered to the printer as electronic prepress files.

Cover Designer: Methodologie, Inc.
Interior Graphic Designer: James D. Kramer
Principal Compositor: Gina Cassill
Electronic Artist: Joel Panchot
Principal Copyeditor: Holly M. Viola
Indexer: Lynn Armstrong

Get a **Free**
e-mail newsletter, updates,
special offers, links to related books,
and more when you

register online!

Register your Microsoft Press® title on our Web site and you'll get a FREE subscription to our e-mail newsletter, *Microsoft Press Book Connections.* You'll find out about newly released and upcoming books and learning tools, online events, software downloads, special offers and coupons for Microsoft Press customers, and information about major Microsoft® product releases. You can also read useful additional information about all the titles we publish, such as detailed book descriptions, tables of contents and indexes, sample chapters, links to related books and book series, author biographies, and reviews by other customers.

Registration is easy. Just visit this Web page and fill in your information:

http://www.microsoft.com/mspress/register

Microsoft®

- -